ONE DAY IN AFGHANISTAN

BASED ON TRUE STORY

Eric Duetchmann

Copyrights © 2024

All rights reserved.

This book many not be reproduced, in whole or in part, including illustrations, in any form (beyond that copying permitted by Sections 107 and 108 in the U.S. Copyright Law and except by reviewers for the public press), without written permission from the publishers.

This book is based on a true story.

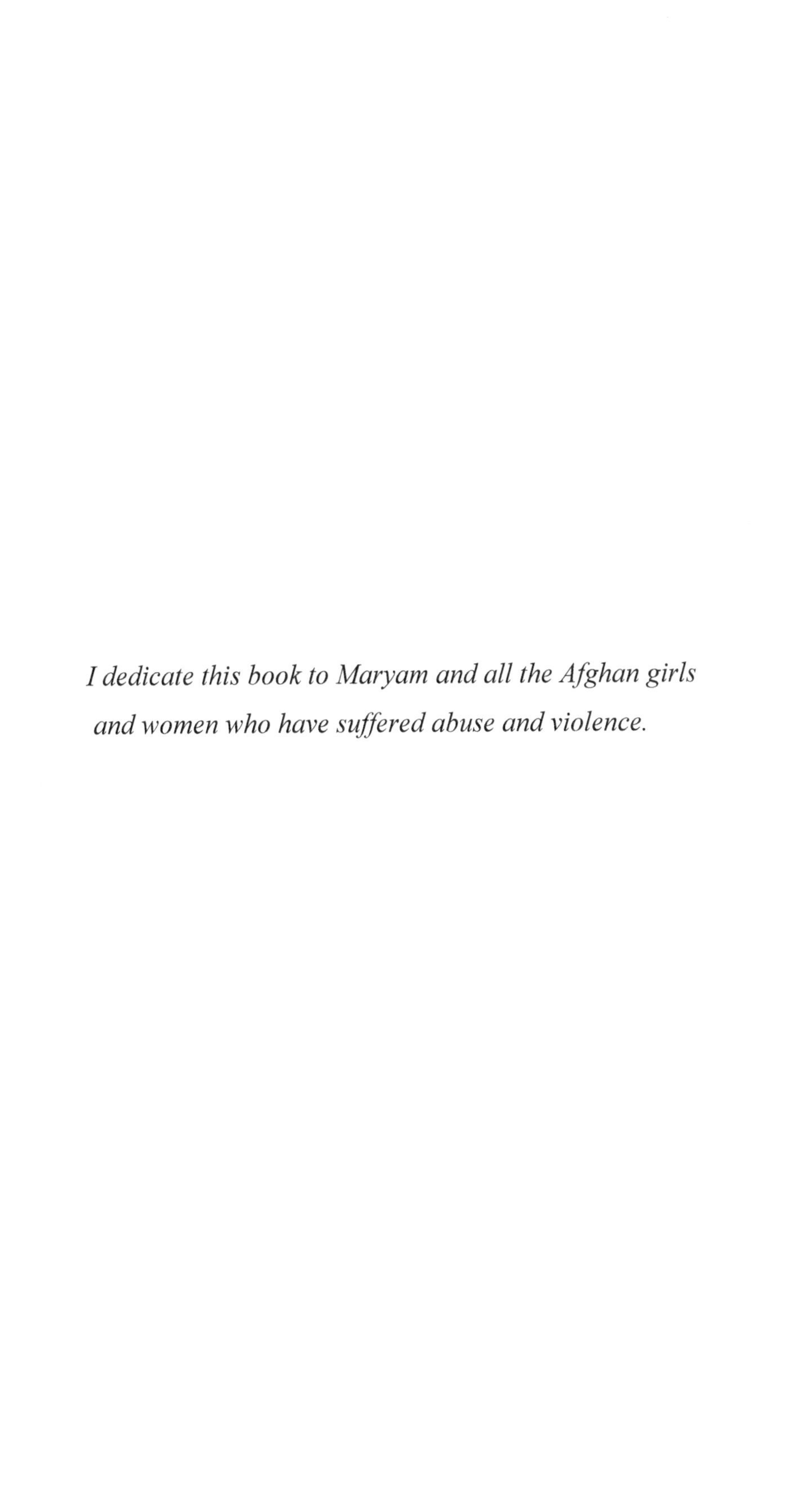

I dedicate this book to Maryam and all the Afghan girls and women who have suffered abuse and violence.

Acknowledgment

I wish to acknowledge all of the Afghans I have met in the last eight years who have given me an in-depth understanding of the Afghan culture, inner workings of extended families, and extensive familial-social networks. I wish to thank the many people who have listened to me retell Maryam's story and those who have read drafts and provided comments in particular, Sonja Richards, who gave a very close reading. I also appreciate the editors at Amazon. I thank Karleigh Kollander for the artwork on the front cover. Her artistic skills reflect deep perception of the world.

I also wish to thank my wife Jennifer. We have been active parents of Maryam for nearly ten years as of this writing. There have been many challenges but the rewards of love far exceed the challenges. Jennifer and I have shared the many ups and downs, tightening the bonds that encircle the three of us. Jennifer has chosen not to be involved with the writing of the book for the most part. However, at the end of the process nearing publication, she guided me through working with the Amazon editors on the front and back covers. She saw things I couldn't see because I am partially color blind!

And, last but not least, I thank Maryam who told me her story in the first place, as hard as it was to tell. The trauma she has endured is exceeded only by the love she gives.

About the Author

Eric Duetchmann and his wife took in a teenage Afghan girl, Maryam. Back in Afghanistan, her brother nearly took her life in an honor killing. She ended up in Canada and got connected with Eric and his wife. In the ensuing eight years, Maryam talked at length about the trauma of her life and that of her family back in Afghanistan. Eric took notes that turned out to be this book.

Table of Contents

Introduction

This book is not for everyone. It has many gruesome, graphic descriptions of disturbing violence. This book is the story of an Afghan girl, Maryam. My wife, Jennifer, and I took Maryam in when she was fifteen years old in 1995, and at the time I have finished this book, she was thirty-nine years old.

Maryam was nearly a victim of a traditional honor killing at the hands of her brother, a concept I still have difficulty grasping. She escaped that attempted killing, fled to Canada, and ended up coming to live with us. Over the course of the first year with us, Maryam unraveled different parts of the attempted honor killing story. Normally, I talk a lot, but that first year she was with us, I shut my mouth and listened. I have had many experiences with widely diverse cultures in India and Africa. Her story exceeded any of those experiences. It was simply gut-wrenching to hear Maryam narrate all of these horrific, real-life events. In addition, Maryam had suppressed many events before she came to Canada because her mind simply could cope with them. They were revealed years later through counseling.

It is precisely because this story is hard to hear that this is a story that needs to be told.

With this book, I seek to raise awareness and compassion because accurate and full information is fundamental to a civil society. And perhaps some readers might act to help in some way. Helping someone you don't know and who is in need is not easy—the greater their need, the more difficult it is to help. The first step is listening compassionately, then conversing. I hope this book starts a conversation.

Most Canadians, I think, have some degree of awareness of Afghanistan since Canada had troops there for thirteen years. (Where I use "Canada," it in most cases also applies to the U.S. but I use just Canada for the sake of consistency.) I have talked with many people about Afghanistan, and one of the first topics is that Afghan men don't treat women very well there, and many respond, "Oh, yea, that's a real problem there. I feel so sorry for those women and girls!" And further, I have been surprised by how many have even more detailed knowledge of the situation in Afghanistan.

During the twenty years of occupation by Western forces from 2001 to 2021, there were many non-profit and non-governmental organizations that provided humanitarian aid to this small country of 40 million people. When the Taliban took in 2021 over, they kicked out virtually all of those non-profits. Help from outside Afghanistan is necessary, but in the end, change must come from within the country, inside the families, and inside the hearts and minds of individual Afghans. Politics within Afghanistan is fraught with complexity as deep as one might find in the world. Fifty years of war imploded the Afghan civilization and has made maintaining a civil society problematic. I think this implosion is a major factor in the violence brought down on Afghan women and girls. The Taliban takeover is, at this writing, driving the implosion deeper, and close observers see nothing on the horizon to change that. The Taliban is a reflection of the deeply rooted tribalism stemming back millennia. One of the worst traditions is honor killing, especially by villagers stoning a girl buried up to her waist.

Helping can be sending some money to a non-governmental organization (NGO) so one Afghan girl can go to school one year longer, to build a school, to educate and build a middle class, to train doctors, nurses, and lawyers, and so forth. All of this will help to rebuild a civil society with rule of law that Afghanistan had before the decades of war. Obviously, with the Taliban takeover, these things are difficult, if not impossible, to do. As of August 2021, the Taliban has restricted girls from going to school past the sixth grade, forbidden women from going to universities, and forbidden women from working for NGO's and similar organizations from Western countries and the United Nations.

The best option I see is to contribute to NGO's that are working to reverse the Taliban policies from locations outside of Afghanistan. A few of these NGO's are Women for Afghan Women, Amnesty International, and Human Rights Watch. Afghan teachers who taught in schools before the Taliban takeover are now teaching online courses. Sarya, a central figure in this book, has been taking online courses with those teachers who formerly taught her in the classroom. Contributing money to advance that education would be an excellent avenue of helping.

In yet another step to oppress girls and women, the Taliban has restricted them from most public places without a male escort, thus leaving them to be in their houses. Also, we heard from Maryam that the Taliban is going door-to-door to find out if any girl seventeen and older is married or not. If they're not, it is the *Taliban that will arraign for husband of their choosing.*

Moving beyond all of the horror stories in this book, I need to make very clear that Maryam has been a treasure in our lives, a blessing. In spite of all of the trauma she has endured, she is infinitely kind, warm, giving, and loving. To have her in our lives is beyond words. Love is reflected in love.

-Eric Deutchmann

Chapter 1: Honor Killing

Maryam's mother says, "You're getting married!"

The year is 1995, and the place is Kunduz, Afghanistan. One day, when Maryam was thirteen, her mother, Shabana, came into her classroom and took her out, something Shabana had never done before. To be more accurate, Shabana physically yanked her out of the classroom.

"Mom, what's going on?"

"You're going to get married."

"What??!!"

"You're going to get married to your cousin, Hafiz. You are going to America."

Hafiz was a distant cousin but still a cousin. (We thought on hearing this, "what about the diversity of the gene pool?") Maryam could not understand what her mother was doing because she had never heard of Hafiz. Shabana had arranged this marriage through one of her sisters, who Maryam calls "the bad aunt". Usually, in Afghan culture, the father arranges the marriage, but for reasons I came to find out only much later, Shabana made the arrangement. The "bad aunt" had an overriding influence over Maryam's mother, and the bad aunt herself abused Maryam terribly also. Maryam never referred to the bad aunt by name, which I interpret as a means, probably unconscious, to minimize her as a person. Also, if Maryam referred to her as "the bad aunt, she must be really bad compared to her sister Shabana.

ONE DAY IN AFGHANISTAN

Hafiz lived in Houston, Texas, and Maryam, of course, had never heard of Texas. Hafiz went over to Afghanistan to meet Maryam and her family, and she was very shocked when she first met him. He was ugly, fat, and old, forty years old, more than twice her age. The first time Hafiz travelled to Afghanistan was to ask her father, Amir, his permission to marry her. Amir didn't like him at all, but the decision of her mother and her bad aunt outweighed Amir's opinion.

There was a big engagement party where everybody was dressed up in very fancy clothes, and the women put a lot of makeup on Maryam. Women put henna on their hands, which is beautiful and decorative but just temporary. It looks like a tattoo, but it's not. In Afghan culture, henna brings good luck and happiness. For Maryam, all of the things she had to go through, the social intensity, was really too much. There is some murkiness as to whether this was an engagement or a marriage and what that meant in Afghanistan or what it meant in Canada Maryam used these terms interchangeably. It was apparently legal under Muslim law but probably not under Canadian law, which made this whole proposition more confusing. Maybe it got lost in translation.

To get Maryam to the Canada, Hafiz requested a marriage visa, for which he needed a birth certificate saying she was sixteen. She was actually thirteen, so Hafiz paid an Afghan attorney to prepare a falsified birth certificate saying she was sixteen. Maryam thought she was sixteen. Later when she entered Canada, the entry document from the Canadian agency that protects the border used that falsified birth certificate, and since then, for more than eight years, I used that as age on all sorts of official documents.

After Maryam was here in Canada with us for a couple of years, Amir was looking through his papers and found her real birth certificate, which showed she was born in 1982, making her thirteen years old (her real age) at the wedding (or engagement). As an aside, even today Afghans commonly are not given birth certificates, another feature of Afghanistan being an ancient third-world country.

After the engagement party, some months had passed, and then it was time for her to fly to Texas. She arrived after a very long, tiring flight, only to find out that Hafiz was not there to meet her. She sat there for two hours, not knowing any English to ask people questions, and she felt very lost and alone. She was crying so hard, she felt so confused, and she couldn't figure out what was happening. What kind of man is this? Finally, *after two hours,* he showed up. Even right from the beginning of this so-called marriage, things were bad between Hafiz and Maryam. Remember, in Afghanistan, the woman is always wrong.

Hafiz was living with his mother and five other family members in a small three-bedroom apartment, making it even more crowded than her home back in Afghanistan. The first night, he said that there was no bedroom for the two of them and that they had to sleep on the couch. She couldn't believe it. This guy was supposed to be some kind of rich American. She thought a new bride and groom were supposed to have their own bedroom. But on the other hand, she told us, "I didn't want to sleep next to him; he was so fat and ugly. The couch in the living room was L-shaped, thank heavens. He took one section, and I took the other."

Hafiz treated Maryam very badly, giving her no respect. His mom and sister treated her nicely, so that was some comfort compared to Hafiz. The two argued constantly. She told him she did not want to have sex until she was eighteen.

He would not stop, and he pushed himself on her many times—that is, he raped her.

Then he said, *"You are not a virgin."*

She said, *"I am a virgin; take me to the doctor, and I will prove it."*

He wouldn't take her, and she never was able to prove to him that she was a virgin. One of their arguments got very bad. They were in the kitchen, and she grabbed one of the big kitchen knives, pointed it at her own stomach, and told him she was going to kill herself. She said, "Then people will think you stabbed me." He backed down, and then she put the knife down. He realized if she had killed herself, he would be a suspect and perhaps would go to jail.

Back to Afghanistan and the attempted "honor killing."

Maryam was with Hafiz only a week, and he said he was going to send her back to Afghanistan, to Kunduz, her hometown. Even though this so-called marriage was pretty much a nightmare, she was shocked. She had just gotten married and had come all the way from Afghanistan to Texas. He said he would follow her back to Afghanistan soon and not to worry. Well, there was a lot to worry about. She was very scared that someone in her family would attempt an honor killing.

In Afghanistan, if a woman is involved in a dispute with a man, it brings dishonor to her family. Someone in the family must punish her for regaining the honor of the family—even to the extent of killing, and this is the essence of honor killing.

Honor killing springs from ancient tribal traditions in Afghanistan about how a woman is treated, which assumes that the woman or girl is always wrong. This is just part of Afghan culture and is something that people from Western cultures simply cannot understand, it is simply unheard of. I have explained this to many Canadians, and they just scratch their head in shock, aghast, and disbelief. However, as with all generalizations, not every Afghan family follows this particular tradition.

Maryam flew back to Kunduz, and many of her family members were there. Her older brother Nargiz came up to her quickly and started to slap her and hit her in the face. They punched her in the stomach, threw her on the floor, and kicked her in her stomach and the back. They kicked her so hard in her back that her kidneys hurt for more than a year afterward. She could in no way defend herself. Nargiz had her down on her back and then started to choke her. After a year of Maryam telling the story of the honor killing, she finally told the final moment when Shabana yelled to Nargiz, *"Kill her, kill her."* She had held back the worst part of the story.

Maryam was getting near to passing out, when this lady appeared, a lady nobody in Maryam's family knew. The woman picked Maryam up and protected her from Nargiz. This woman shouted at them, *"You are not even animals. Even animals wouldn't treat each other this bad."* This woman was an angel. Somehow, this woman got Maryam away from Nargiz and out of the airport. She took Maryam to her house and nursed Maryam's wounds as best she could. Maryam was bruised and hurt all over. The lady fed Maryam and let her rest and sleep.

Onto Kabul

After a few days, Maryam gained enough strength to travel, and the lady put Maryam on the regular Afghan bus, meaning old and rickety, going from Kunduz to Kabul, about six hours away on a very bumpy road. Robbers, bandits, and kidnappers frequented this road, adding one more element of danger. But in Afghanistan, life was filled with many risks. Women faced an especial danger on that road, sometimes being raped. She finally arrived in Kabul, fortunately unharmed.

Maryam was wearing a black burka (see Appendix 3), which is an enveloping outer garment that fully covers the body and the face. A mesh covers the eyes so the woman or girl wearing it can see out, but seeing in is fully obscured. Nobody could tell how young she was or how beat up she was. Here she was, this short figure in this black burka—what a scene. When she got to Kabul, she had this little phone book, and the only person she knew there was Sayeed. He had gotten engaged to Maryam's older sister Jamila about a month before, and Maryam hadn't even met him yet. On the phone, he asked in a panic, "Where are you?" He got there as fast as he could go and saw that Maryam was all beaten up and looked horrible. He was just terrified at her sight. Somehow, Shabana figured out Maryam was in Kabul. Shabana also knew that Maryam probably knew just one person in Kabul, Sayeed. Shabana called Sayeed and told him she wanted to come to Kabul and help Maryam, and she asked for his address. The actual reason she wanted the address is so she could send Nargiz there to kill Maryam. Sayeed said he would give the address, but said that he needed $4,000 first. Shabana sold some jewelry and sent the $4,000, and then Sayeed didn't give the address—he *foiled her plot.*

Sayeed picked a small hotel off of the main roads where Nargiz was not likely to find them. She felt so much safer that

Sayeed was protecting her. Very often over the years with us, she would say, "Sayeed is the best man I have ever known, he watched over me day and night." She would often repeat, "He never tried to have sex with me or touch me in a bad way. That is not how any ordinary Afghan boy would treat a girl."

Shabana sold many more expensive jewels and sent him another $6,000, making the total $10,000. With the $10,000 he bought Maryam a visa and a plane ticket to Canada. She already had her passport from when she went to Texas less than a week before. Sayeed did this all within two weeks, and that was no doubt partly why it cost so much. Sayeed has very high morals, but in this case, he would compromise for a greater cause, correcting a wrong to a right. He dealt with some shady characters in the process. Maryam never explained those details, and maybe she didn't even know. Maryam said she was so nervous about Nargiz trying to chase her down to kill her, she hardly ate or drank or even slept for two weeks. When you get beat up like she had, it's only natural to be driven by such real fear—not paranoia or an imaginary fear, but real fear.

Here is this small girl trying to escape from her brother, who is large and trying to finish her off with this honor killing. She was so scared. She never imagined an honor killing would come into her life. Sayeed and Maryam thought the best way to protect her was to get her to another country for sure. The United States was the best choice for a lot of reasons, but maybe if she went to Canada, it would be less likely that Nargiz would find her. So Canada it was. For years we were fearful of Nargiz finding Maryam, and us.

Chapter 2: Onto Canada

Flying to Canada and going through border control

The month prior to arriving in Canada simply exhausted Maryam emotionally and physically. There was the trip from Afghanistan through Seoul, South Korea to Texas travelling twenty hours and half-way around the world. After that fateful week in Texas, she returned to Kunduz on another flight of twenty hours. Then of course her brother, Nargiz, nearly killed her. Then the two weeks in the hotel in Kabul she barely ate, drank, or slept out of fear that Nargiz would find her and kill her. Finally, the flight with a stop in Istanbul, Turkey, and onto Toronto, Canada another twenty hours half-way around the world, in the opposite direction. That's a lot to go through—she was rung out.

An Afghan woman who spoke Farsi was on the same flight to Toronto that Maryam was on. At this point, Maryam knew no English and needed all of the help she could get. This woman said she would help her by holding her passport and visa. Maryam was so exhausted, so drained, she was in this strange land, and didn't really understand what you needed to do to come into a foreign country. And she was so young. Maryam accepted the woman's offer, thinking she was just being helpful. When Maryam got to the border control station, they asked where her passport and visa were. She said she gave them to this lady who by that time, had disappeared. The border control agents put her directly into a "detention facility," which Maryam definitively said was "really a jail."

They asked Maryam if she knew anyone in Canada. She said not in Canada, but she knew Hafiz in Texas, and she gave them Hafiz's phone number. They called, Hafiz answered, and they asked if he knew Maryam. At first, he said, "Yes" and then he quickly said, "Oh, no, no, I've never heard of her." Maryam could hear this conversation and couldn't believe it. He knew exactly what he was doing. He was just leaving her in this this jail cell. This was her husband—they had just gotten married a month ago. She was in Canada, a land of the free, but for her, she was in jail—alone, very alone. Maryam told us, "All I had for clothes was my burka."

This woman who stole Maryam's passport and visa also asked if she could help her by taking care of her one large suitcase which had all of her possessions for her new life in Canada. At first, Maryam said "no" she would take care of it herself. The woman pressed Maryam further and convinced her it would make things easier. The woman ended up stealing Maryam's suitcase, too, and that is why she had no other clothes. It had pictures of Maryam's family, her only remembrances of her family. In the ensuing year, Maryam would frequently ask where her suitcase was. We contacted the airport and the airlines, but they had no record of the suitcase. This was sad because what she wanted most was pictures of her family.

There were two women jailers at the border control station. One spoke Farsi, Maryam's native language. She was rough and mean to Maryam and said, "*They should send you back to Afghanistan.*" Maryam was thinking, "Here I am, I'm *in Canada*, and this woman says they should send me back?! After all, I had gone through to get to Canada, and this woman says I should go back?!" And on top of it, *the Farsi-speaking jailer was an Afghan!* The other jailer was a black woman, and Maryam said she was nice and saw to it within her power that Maryam did not go back to Afghanistan.

They told her to take a shower, and then they gave her jail clothes. They offered her food, and she ate a whole bunch right away because she had eaten very little for the two weeks she was with Sayeed while he protected her. Later, she found out it was pork. She could not believe that she had eaten pork because eating pig flesh is clearly forbidden by Islamic dietary laws. Years later, Maryam would talk about that event because it was just such a bizarre event for her. She says it was a little funny that she ate pork and didn't know it. Come to Canada and eat pork? After all of the intense trauma and here was a little comic relief.

The jail cell was small and had just a little window. It scared her so much. There was no doubt it was a real jail. She later found out the jail was called a "detention center" by the government. Maryam said, "Right, it's a detention center—*it's a jail.*" Maryam had no idea what was going to happen to her. How long would she be in jail? She knew no one in Canada. The next day, the detention people drove her and some others about three hours to another jail. This apparently was from the detention center near the airport to another, larger detention center. Again, she had no idea how long this would last. Each hour and each day seemed like forever.

Light for Youth

On the third day, some people came and drove her to another place for about two hours. It was not a jail. It had a lot of nice buildings on a large amount of land. She had no idea what this place was. Many adult people smiled at her, and she felt exceptionally welcomed. There was one man, somewhat older than the other adults, who came over to her, put his hand on her head, and said in English, of course, "You will be safe here." She of course didn't understand his English, but she could feel through his kind smile and warm heart what he was saying. *"You will be safe here."* Now, she knew she would be safe at this place. Safety was a very big deal, of course. For nearly a month, she was really, really *not safe*. She says, even years after the event, "I will remember that forever. All that horrible stuff with Hafiz, the honor killing, fear of Nargiz, the jail—that was behind me! I didn't think anything even close to this place would be possible."

This place she found out was called Light for Youth, or LFY, a Christian-based, non-profit program helping youth-at-risk, kids who have dysfunctional families or no family, kids with parents on drugs or in jail, trafficked girls (many from Central American countries), kids from juvenile jails, and the like. The kindly man would say, "You will be safe here" to every one of these kids because they came from places in life where it was not safe in one way or another. But Maryam, with her own story was much different. LFY was linked up with border control in international airports where undocumented, under-eighteen youth might show up. The border control agents would notify LFY (and programs like it), and LFY would come pick them up.

They provided a translator for Maryam, who explained the basics of how things would work at this new place. But the translator could not be there all of the time, so mostly, she had to figure things out on her own. The adults who worked there helped her a lot, too. Maryam is exceptionally outgoing and has a strong desire to communicate. Even in the beginning, with no English words, she used hand gestures and body English. She got one word, and then another and quickly built up a functional vocabulary. There were about a hundred girls and a hundred boys, mostly teenagers. The place had a lot of land, about two hundred acres. The boys lived in houses on one side of the area and the girls on the other. They lived in houses that looked like Canadian single-family houses in a single-family subdivision. There were big houses, big enough to fit about 8 to 10 girls. They had 24/7 staff supervision, with at least one staff present in the house at all times to make sure the girls behaved. There were white, black, and Hispanic girls. But Maryam was different; she was from Afghanistan. No one had ever even heard about Afghanistan. Because of her brownish skin color and black hair, they thought she was Hispanic until they heard her first word. When we first met Maryam after she had been there eight months, she was speaking Spanglish with a Hispanic accent. Our first meetings were once a week for three hours, and *she could converse intelligibly for all three of those hours after only eight months in Canada!* One of the things LFY did for Maryam was to give her a physical to check her general health. They discovered she was pregnant, which Maryam didn't realize. Soon after that, she delivered a stillborn baby. This could well be because she was exceptionally traumatized during the previous month. Part of that was Hafiz repeatedly raping her.

At LFY, in the house where Maryam was living, there was this girl, Angela. She was friendly with Maryam, and Maryam thought okay, she will take all the friends she can get. After a couple of weeks, Angela said to Maryam, "I love you." Maryam thought it was nice that someone said they loved her. Then Angela pushed it and said passionately, "I *love* you." Then Maryam realized what was going on and freaked out. This was something that just did not happen in Afghanistan. Maryam kind of knew of the idea of homosexuality but *never* experienced it in real life. Angela even kept kissing Maryam and touching her in inappropriate ways, which *really* freaked her out. There were cameras all over the place and staff on duty 24/7, enabling the staff and everyone at LFY to know what was going on with Angela going after Maryam.

When you turned eighteen at LFY you "age out", and you must leave the program. LFY was funded in part with government grants, and that was one of the requirements of the grant. Maryam was turning eighteen, and LFY wanted to find a family for her. There was no way Maryam was ready to go out into the world on her own. Her language skills were rudimentary and not good enough to negotiate employment and support herself financially. She didn't know anyone in Canada. Also, this thing with Angela made it that much more urgent. The pressure to get out of LFY was just one more layer of stress on top of all the other things that happened to her before she got to LFY. It was all too much, and she was only too glad to get out of there.

It took Maryam over a year to tell all of the details leading up to and the immediate aftermath of the attempted honor killing. She would tell the story over again and again unravelling nuances and bigger features of the story. But there was one major point of the events which she didn't tell us until toward the end of the first year. It was when Nargiz had her down on her back and then started to choke her, and Shabana yelled to Nargiz, *"Kill her, kill her."* Maryam just couldn't tell us that part because it was the most traumatic crescendo of the whole string of events.

ONE DAY IN AFGHANISTAN

Taking in a seventeen-year-old Afghan girl

When Jennifer and I tell people about Maryam, their first question is, "How did you guys get connected?" Answering this goes all the way back in our lives, starting in the 1960's when Jennifer and I lived in the small town of High Prairie, Alberta, Canada. It was near the Kapawe'no First Nation, which is an equivalent of an Indian reservation in the U.S. There were all these Indian kids with parents who suffered from alcoholism and often in jail and who otherwise did not have nurturing parents and families. They would find a non-Indian family that was emotionally healthy and take them as their de facto parents. Mind you, this was a low bar to meet. If you're not in jail, you've met the first qualification. This was similar to the situation with Maryam. If you're not abusive, you're good to go. There were these three Indian girls, about ten years old, there who did just that with us. They spent a lot of their free time with us, and it was this instant family.

We moved from High Prairie to Toronto in 1990, where I would run into kids, mostly kids ten to fourteen years old, with single moms, we knew who could use a father figure. I would do lots of different things with these kids, whatever worked—go to festivals, play table games, do one-on-one sports, watch them play sports—just give them some attention, which really would fill a big hole in their lives. It's just in my blood. In the 1970's and 1980's we housed several college-age students, anywhere from a week to two years. It went beyond saving them money for them—we once again became family. When we were in Toronto, a local TV station had a five-minute program called Wednesday's Child, focusing on a child in need of adoption or foster home. All they needed was a nurturing family. I would just end up crying my eyes out. But Jennifer would caution me that *she* was not ready and that we had taken in self-sufficient college-age students for a limited time, not younger kids to adopt long-term.

In 1994, we decided to open our house up to a college-age student once more. We had bought this four-bedroom, three-bathroom house so Jennifer's mom could live with us. She had a bedroom, a sitting room, and her own bathroom. Jennifer's mom would go back and forth from High Prairie to Vancouver, British Columbia, where Jennifer had grown up and still had a family. Six months with us and six months in Vancouver with her brother and sister. But she got to the point where she couldn't fly back and forth, and she decided to stay in Vancouver. That opened up a bedroom with its own bathroom.

In November 1994, Jennifer had let the word out through a women's church group that our door was open. One of the women in the group was Carol. She and her husband had a long history of housing all sorts of people, and Teresa, who was a good friend of their daughters growing up. Teresa was working for this non-profit, Light for Youth (LFY). In January 1995, less than two months later, LFY called and said they had a seventeen-year-old Afghan girl in need of a family—two degrees of separation! The first thing we heard about this young Afghan girl was that she just barely escaped from being killed by her brother through this thing called an "honor killing," which we found out later more fully what that meant. She had a family member who did not adhere to any such tribal customs who spirited her out of Afghanistan to Toronto. I was in Yellowknife, Northwest Territories, in the Arctic part of Canada, on a work trip. Jennifer called me, told me this girl's story, and asked me if I was ready to take this seventeen-year old girl in. Without hesitation, I said, "Yes!" For Jennifer and me, this was instinctive. She wasn't a college-age student and probably not self-sufficient, but that didn't matter—she was special.

Maryam told us later that one day, her case worker asked her if she wanted Canadian parents. She exclaimed, *"What?! Can this be? Canadian parents?"*

It was beyond her comprehension. "Do they have a son?" Meaning if there was a son in the house that was a deal breaker. Nargiz's attempt at honor killing was the most traumatic thing in her life, so a young male in a close relationship was not going to happen. In February, we met with the LFY staff to start the process of a national and provincial police background check and getting us approved, which they are required to do for adoptions. We were not planning to adopt Maryam but rather to just "take her in," house her, feed her, and financially support her. Because she was on the verge of turning eighteen, it meant adoption wouldn't have been necessary. But LFY had us go through a process as if we were adopting her, which is a good thing on both sides.

By mid-March, the background checks were completed, and we went out to meet her for the first time. They had a main building with classrooms, chapel, cafeteria, and a library. The library was a big space with a large U-shaped table. We walked in, and sitting at the table were her current casework, her previous case worker, and a couple of administrators. It was like a semi-official panel that was more formal than we expected. We talked some. They explained how LFY works in arranging for the kids to be taken in by a family. We explained why and how we had opened our house and home to take Maryam in and our general background.

The moment of the meeting

The moment is close. Jennifer and I feel anxiety mounting. Who will this girl be? Is she tall or short? Will she even look at us? Will she be calm or scared? Teresa told us that she was very friendly and very outgoing and knew everyone, even from the beginning when she knew no English. Does she hug or not be into touching? She walked in and rushed toward us, and the three of us hugged, and all three of us were just crying. It was an instant family. We had no idea what the future would be with Maryam. The three of us were just living in the moment. It is a moment that Jennifer, Maryam, and I will never forget. We melded instantly. She needed us in so many ways, and we found that we needed her. People say, "You took her in. What a great thing you are doing for her." And we say, "We could do nothing else. If you saw somebody thrown into a ditch, you don't walk by. You extend your hand and pull her out." We were helping her, but by the same token, she was a blessing to us, filling our hearts with a lot of love. Now, it's eight years later, and we are still a family this nuclear family of three grew by connecting to extended families on both sides. We were not looking for a seventeen-year-old Afghan girl with no family in Canada, with needs to adjust to Canadian culture, with a need to better understand English to function in an English-speaking world, and who greatly needs to heal from the huge emotional trauma she had suffered in Afghanistan.

LFY had a system to introduce the youth to the prospective parents over a set period of time—time to give both sides the opportunity to back out if it looked like the relationship wouldn't work. In the beginning, we had visits to

LFY for three hours on Sunday afternoons. On the first visit to our house, she gave us and the house a detailed inspection. She walked around and picked up things, and looked them over. When we showed her her own bedroom and bathroom, she almost collapsed. In Afghanistan, she was one of eight kids who slept in one room side by side with the parents on each end, *and they had one bathroom for all ten of them plus frequent family visits.* Then, we had overnight visits. Any of us could have backed out of the arrangement, but it didn't happen. The love continued from that very first sight onward.

Another big day came, May 10, 1996, when Maryam moved in. It so happened that it was Mothers' Day, which was special and prophetic. We joke that she was born for a second time, and she came out as an eighteen-year-old. Moving her belongings from LFY was quite an exercise. She had several new suitcases which LFY bought for her. Everything else was in about ten large plastic garbage bags. There were so many that we had to come back for two more loads—way more stuff than when she arrived at the airport with only a burqa on her back! LFY had so much money to shower on these kids. They bought them all these nice clothes from pretty nice stores. Once moved in, Maryam was extremely happy to have her own bedroom and bathroom.

For many months after having moved out of LFY, she would talk from time to time about how glad she was to get out of LFY. But when we went back for her graduation from their education program, all of the teachers, caseworkers, counselors, cooks, administrators—they all came up and hugged her and asked how she was doing and told her English was coming along very well. Maryam told us, "Yeah, LFY did a lot of good things for me, *they loved me.* I didn't get that back home, especially from my mom."

First weeks and signing up for ESL

In her first week with us, the attorneys had scheduled an appointment with the federal office, which handles asylum applications. We got all the way down there and found out that they had postponed it. She was very emotionally charged because she knew how important this was, so that was a big letdown. Getting approved for asylum would allow her to stay in Canada and not have to go back to Afghanistan and face the threat of honor killing by Nargiz. A year after asylum, she would then receive her permission to work (same as the Green Card in the U.S.), and five more years, she would get Canadian citizenship. We drove to a Mexican restaurant near our house with fun Mexican décor. The great food helped assuage our disappointment with the postponement.

For the rest of May, Maryam mostly spent time in her room. I asked her if she was okay with that, should we find some things to do outside of her room? She said no, it was okay. I realized much later that she was decompressing from all of the events of the previous year, starting with Hafiz, the attempted honor killing, and the time adjusting to LFY and to Canada. At the end of May, Maryam and I went to the local community college to register her for English as a second language (ESL) classes. We looked through the catalogue of courses, and there were the ESL classes. I asked the registration staff on three different visits, and every time they said we had to go to an orientation on a certain day and time and a certain location.

We went and it was in a room that was very warm and packed with about thirty mostly young people who were there to sign up for courses for the first time. The youngest one had a parent with them, as I was doing with Maryam. The orientation leader spoke, seemingly on and on, and the room got hot, and we just wanted to get out of there, but we had to stay so we could register for the classes. He finally finished. Then, the next thing is one-on-one consultations about how to register for their specific classes. There are only two staff and they start on the other side of the room. The room is getting hotter and hotter.

I was really not liking it, and Maryam says, "I want an education, but this is a lot to go through." I thought, "I'm seventy years old, worked in a lot of bureaucracies, even the Federal government, for over twenty-five years, and this is one of the most painful bureaucratic experiences of my life!" Finally, they got to us, and the staff person said, "Oh, you're in the wrong program." It turns out there are two types of ESL classes: those in the regular, main college where English-speaking classes are taught and others in the "Work Force Development Program" in a building separate from the main campus. They have their own registration!

Maryam and I walked out of the hot, hot room and walked by the registration area that has open counters where students can talk with registration staff. It turns out that the head of the registration office is there, and we tell him what we had just gone through. He says, "Oh yeah, you should never have come here. You should have gone to the other place, across the two parking lots." I protested, "I came down here three times, and your underlining staff never got us going to the right place!" It took the chief of registration to find the correct information. The underlying lackies just hadn't got the memo. What a hassle!!! I had to remind myself, "I'm a new dad…of a teenage girl…who is learning English…and other stuff."

A new "friend."

Maryam started her ESL classes in early June 1996, less than a month after she had moved in with us. Our next-door neighbors were a mother and adult daughter. Neither of them worked, so they ended up with a lot of time, and for some of that time, they were looking out of the front window. One day, the daughter called us and said she saw Maryam and a guy get out of the car and go in and out of our house. This was on a Sunday when Jennifer and I had driven up to Ottawa to visit our daughter and her family for the day. We invited Maryam, but she said she'd rather stay home. We left a bit early to find out what was going on. The conversation went like this.

"Maryam, what was going on?"

"Oh, nothing."

"We heard there was some guy here."

"Who did you hear that from? [In an angry and defensive tone.]"

"Don't worry about that. Who was this guy?"

"There's no guy."

This goes back and forth with no answer, and finally fesses up.

"He's a guy I met at the college."

"Was he an Afghan?"

"Yes."

"Did he speak English?"

"Yes."

"What were you guys doing?"

"He was helping me study for my English."

"Anything else?"

"No, he was just helping me with my English."

"Why didn't you tell us what you were doing? Why didn't you go with us?"

"I didn't think you would approve."

"Were you hiding this date because you knew you were going to do something we didn't approve of?"

"Oh…no, no, not anything like that."

It goes back and forth more. We push her. She breaks down crying, contritely. This was our first experience of becoming a new parent, figuring out how to do it, and, in this case, setting boundaries. So Jennifer and I made it very clear what she could and could not do. So the next morning, she comes downstairs to my office, where I am sitting at my desk. I turn in my chair, and she stands in front of me with her hands on her hips, and she says wagging her head and in full body English, throwing her body back and forth defiantly and says, *"Well, Dad, I just cannot do this boundary thing."* I think to myself, "We've got a strong-willed, stubborn, and wild child on our hands. The future is going to be interesting." And that turned out to be true.

ESL classes

ESL classes and homework go on through the summer and fall of 2015. She takes the studies seriously, and we help her with the homework. While at LFY, they sent her to a community college near them to take initial ESL so she could learn the Roman alphabet and read from left to right. Farsi is an Arabic type of script, and they read from right to left. The ESL classes have many levels of proficiency and the four categories are reading, writing, speaking, and listening. Maryam is very gregarious, a characteristic that accelerates learning a second language. If you're shy, you won't pick up the new language nearly as fast. Maryam was enthusiastic and having fun. One time, we helped her write a one-page paper about taking a vacation to Montreal and what she would see. This got into her head because we were planning a trip there the following spring. She looked up information online, doing actual research. That would seem simple to a first language speaker, but for a second-language speaker, it's a big deal. She also practiced making an oral presentation in front of Jennifer and me. She's definitely not shy, but the idea of making a formal presentation in front of us was definitely a bit challenging. Then, to take the next step and make it in front of her twelve-student class was another. She practiced and got it together.

The first rule of class is no phones. In each class, it always seemed there were boys who wanted to use their phones and talk and disrupt during class, which frustrated her no end. The three of us couldn't figure out why you would pay good money for the class and then just blow it off. Youthful indiscretion, I think. Maryam got in the habit of sitting in the front row to avoid any boys whenever possible. They would just bother her whenever they had a chance, which was the beginning of unwanted male attention, leading to sexual harassment. However, this kind of harassment was mild compared to how girls and women are treated in Afghanistan. LFY was giving her a scholarship which ended up totaling $12,000 for six semesters. This is one more example of how well-funded LFY was and how generous they were to these youth who needed help. This was the focus of her energy and ours for that summer, fall, and going into 1998.

Social media, paperwork, storytelling

LFY allowed her to call home for twenty minutes every other week. We felt it was a good idea for her to have a phone so she could keep in touch with her family. Jennifer and I thought, here she has been ripped out of her family in a most horrific way. She should be able to keep in touch with her family. Our intent had merit, but there were and are many pitfalls, social media being what it is. Jennifer said, *"No Facebook!"* Yeah, right, like we're going to be able to watch every little keystroke. There are different kinds of apps that enable talking, texting, and videoing *to Kunduz Afghanistan, on the other end of the world in a remote place in a remote country, and all for free!* It was well into my adulthood by the time computers became widely available and I'm generally slow on the uptake of new technology. The accelerating pace of new communication technology still boggles my mind. Maryam started using that phone a lot of time every day,calling back home an hour a day on the average. It's eight years later, and that's still the average enabling total connection to her Afghan family. In the early years she mostly talked with her mother, then it shifted to others in her family. The most trying and difficult part of this is that her family is beset with lots of traumatic events which then translates to trauma for her. I mean *a lot of trauma.*

I helped Maryam with a lot of paperwork: signing up for ESL courses, filing for reimbursement for tuition with LFY, getting different cards (a social security card, ID like a driver's license, permit to work), government benefits, job applications, taxes, making doctor's appointments, going with her to appointments to translate complicated words, and so on. It became a mental burden and stressful for me. I had my full-time day job, and this became like another full-time job. If she was our own Canadian daughter speaking English as a first language, born with Canadian citizenship, not needing government assistance and the like, that would be one thing. As the years have gone by, many of those needs have declined, and she has gradually become more competent in English and more capable of handling her own affairs. She has become strong in oral communication but still has a way to go in writing and reading. Everyone has their own aptitudes and inclinations.

In the first year or so, we were very concerned Nargiz would find us through some Afghan contact in Canada and then come to finish off the honor killing. Whether a real or unreal fear, the three of us were very scared of that possibility. You cannot imagine the lengths we went to prevent that. Our rules: No Facebook, shut down every kind of social media, and do not let your phone number out. We ended up changing her phone number five times in less than a year. We told her mother Shabana not to give it to anyone else, but she kept on doing it. Then Maryam would be getting calls from the Ukraine, Canada, Australia. Finally, Shabana got the message. This was an early inkling that Shabana was not totally bolted down. However, Maryam was still on Facebook and other social media, as are most young people.

Maryam talked every night at dinner for a year to tell the whole story of the attempted honor killing, events before, during, and after—all of the major twists of the path and small but important nuances. Jennifer and I listened intently, in sheer shock, often just crying our eyes out. Then she would weave things in that happened to other young girls, unimaginable, often gut-wrenchingly grisly. Before Maryam, I would easily dominate a conversation because I thought what I had to say was more interesting than the person I was talking with. However, with Maryam's story, I shut my mouth and just sat and listened because I was so spell-bound. Her story was leagues ahead of anything I had experienced before. She had something to say.

I read Maryam's 500-page asylum application, prepared by top-notch attorneys at a world-class law firm working *pro bono*. About a hundred pages were information exclusively about her. It had a translation of Shabana's statement of events prior to Maryam's coming to Canada, her birth certificate, Hafiz's Facebook page, and forms with a lot of details from the federal border control agency.

Then, the attorneys had collected an extensive amount of material, about four hundred pages, about the status of women and girls in Afghanistan from a wide variety of sources, twenty-five in all. They did this to demonstrate that Maryam's strife-torn life was consistent with what happens to women and girls in the broader Afghan society. A cultural determinate that women should work only at home is fundamental. Along with that is the wearing of a hijab or a burka in public is a step up from that. There is a prevalent custom that a male family member escorts a girl or young woman. Women and girls face a lot of violence. At the far end of the scale is an honor killing punishment, the price a woman or girl would have to pay merely because she lived in Afghanistan. I summarize the source material from those four hundred pages in Appendix 1.

Spaghetti bowl

One of the first things Maryam explained to us, even before she moved in, was that she had a hundred and forty cousins. As we came to find out she knows what is going on with a large proportion of them—who got married, who got divorced, who's having a baby, who is arguing with whom, etc., etc. I call this phenomenon the "spaghetti bowl." If one pulls the end of one noodle it will cause movement at the other end of the plate, with sometimes good consequences and, too often, bad ones. It can have to do with something that just happened, or it can be a long standing tribal feud and vendettas. This proved to be true again and again over the eight years Maryam has been in our lives. Maryam's knowledge of world geography is above average for Canadians because of the knowledge gained by keeping track of all of these relatives. One time, she was on an eight-way phone FaceTime conversation with eight cousins in eight different countries. Wow! In Canada, there are concentrations of Afghan-Canadians in Toronto, Montreal, and Vancouver. In the U.S. they are in New York City, Northern Virginia, Fremont, California, Los Angles, and Houston. There are Afghans in dozens of countries around the world. In one of the first conversations I had with her, she told me about getting together with fifteen or so of her cousins and swimming in this creek which had "nasty water." Connecting with a very extended family is just the nature of the culture. Only as time passed did I come to understand more fully what the spaghetti bowl meant—the concept was more true than I could have imagined.

Maryam explained how far and wide communications and socializing work in her very extended Afghan family and friends. Social connections are the strands and cords that hold this tribal society together. For the most part, in Western, industrial society, family ties are not as tight and thick. A major exception is large, extended Hispanic families. At any given meal or throughout the day, there would be her siblings with several of their children and possibly some cousins and aunts and uncles constantly coming and going like a swarm of people ebbing and flowing. One variation on the theme is women of several generations gathering together just to talk or have a meal. One of my favorite pictures of nearly thirty women, sitting on pillows at a long table with fifteen on a side with delicious foods up and down the table and the women all dressed up. Cell phones have extended the geographic reach of communication. They are constantly talking on the phone within Afghanistan and to any of the many countries where the Afghan diaspora has taken up residence. Countries I hear about most frequently are Germany, Turkey, Canada, England (particularly London), Australia, and of course, the U.S. The Afghan population in far-off New Zealand got into the news when there was a mass killing at a mosque a few years ago, and a Muslim who confronted him was from Afghanistan. Maryam found out this particular fact by phone before it came out on the news, which demonstrates how tight and fast the spaghetti bowl works. The spaghetti bowl communications have often worked ahead of the news media. This is another example of the spaghetti bowl phenomenon in action.

This story demonstrates how the local spaghetti bowl works in administering justice. Amir, Maryam's father, heard a hard knocking on the door. He looked out, and there was a large crowd of the neighbors who said Nargiz had been stealing from them and that *the family must leave the neighborhood.* In other words, this is a tribal justice system, not a formal government judicial system, but it worked at least as effectively. Amir was so embarrassed and pleaded with them to let the family take care of things and that he would punish Nargiz. Nargiz had brought shame on the family, and nothing was worse than family shame. Nargiz didn't return home for over a week, at which time Amir beat him severely. Maryam thinks this may have been when bad blood started between Amir and Nargiz. Nargiz was fourteen when this happened. This societal shame is another example of how highly interwoven the very extended Afghan families and society is.

Here's a story of how Jennifer and I got ensnared in the spaghetti bowl. Shabana accidentally tipped a pot of boiling water down half of her body, giving her severe burns. They took her to the hospital and dressed her wounds. A week or two later, her burn wounds were getting worse, and the doctors decided she needed a skin graft. The doctors put her in a coma so they could operate. Amir felt guilty about all the bad things he had said to Shabana over the years. The operation is going to cost $9,000, and many of the extended family chipped in. Even the rich brother of Amir gave $100 (big deal), and the bad aunt, who is also rich gave $200 (another big deal). They asked Maryam for $3,000, knowing she would have to ask me for that. I said, no, that's just too much, perhaps $1,000. The next day, I changed my mind and said, no, just $500. There had to be other relatives who could pay up. Then, there was an uncle on her dad's side that she knew of but never even met, and he was rich. He and Amir got on the phone, and they lambasted Maryam for not coming up with $3,000. Maryam was devastated for days, embarrassed she had dishonored the family, even though I was the one who made the decision to give less. The spaghetti noodles are strong and can be yanked hard enough to extend even to Jennifer and me on the outer rim of the bowl.

LFY asks Maryam to give a speech

Each year, the LFY staff picks out one of their young people whose story particularly tells the benefactors that LFY is really helping the youth who need the help. It was after Maryam had been with us for about six months LFY asked her to come to a fundraiser to give a talk about the honor killing story. Maryam was reluctant because telling the story meant reliving it, and she really didn't want to do that. She didn't want to retraumatize herself. But we told her that telling her story to people who want to donate to LFY will drive home the point that LFY improves the lives of many young people. She thought that sounded good and decided to give the talk. LFY has two major fundraisers a year. The venue was in the ballroom of the Ritz Carlton Hotel, one of the poshest hotels in one of the richest areas in the country. They told us that donors, small and large, would be coming. My sense was that, although they were wealthy, none were haughty, just down to earth, intent on giving to a good cause. They were there to give their money for a program to nurture young ones who have not been nurtured before.

Most programs like LFY are run on a shoestring, but not LFY. Two men founded LFY and started with a few trailers on a 200-acre farm just beyond exurbia which the one man donated. The other co-founder was a good-spirited Christian man, wealthy and good-hearted. These two men were well-connected to fellow-rich people. Consequently, LFY was very well funded and provided the young people going through its doors with every educational and material thing a child could want. They had teachers and classes so they could keep up with their studies, counselors, advisors, overseers in the residential houses, cooks, and so on. They set boundaries to provide behavioral guardrails, which was very important, where most had no boundaries before. But more so, LFY gave them boundless love.

When we walked into the ballroom, it was so large it was overwhelming. It was then we found out it holds six hundred people! Waiters and waitresses were there setting up the tables. To get the feel of it, Maryam got up on the platform, stepped to the podium, and started speaking into the microphone. Hearing her voice fill the room just about knocked us out. It was so loud and resonant and deep across the room. She ran through the speech a few times, and then she stopped to take a rest. It was about another hour until people started coming in.

As people were coming in, one of the people we talked with was a woman who, as it turned out, was chairperson of the LFY Board and her husband. They were wonderful people, as one might expect. They knew of Maryam's story and expressed compassion. they personally had taken in a teen-age girl from LFY, gave her every material thing, and as always, nurtured her with love. They had lots of money, so that was not a problem. Within six months, she disappeared and they were crushed. They felt they had done everything right. Helping tender young souls who have been damaged emotionally is no easy task. In fact, it is not easy bringing up your own flesh and blood children, and have a healthy, nourishing home for starters. Maryam had her own monumental post-traumatic stress disorder (PTSD), but she did not run away. She really had nowhere to run. We were the only stable thing to hang onto. She had absolutely no social network to run to, and her language skills were not good enough to enable her to run away. Generally, it was easy to stay where she had a roof over her head, got fed, and felt secure.

In preparing Maryam's talk, Maryam and I picked out words Maryam could pronounce and words that were intelligible with her accent. Practicing got tedious because the LFY staff member who worked with us would discard the script Maryam and I prepared and pulled out his own script that told some story that was not Maryam's story.

Back to the ballroom. Early on with Maryam I would just think about even a small piece of her story, and I would just start bawling. But at this point, I thought I could think about her story and not cry. Then hundreds people started filling up the ballroom, eight persons to a round table each. Linen tablecloths and napkins. Food served by waiters and waitresses in black and white formal wear. I kept on feeling, this room was so huge. They placed us by the platform where she was to speak. The choreography was that after Maryam was done, Jennifer and I would step up on the platform, get introduced briefly as her Canadian parents, and then the three of us would step down.

The speech

The time came for Maryam to give her speech. She stepped up to the podium and the microphone. Maryam is short, so they had a small booster platform, so she could reach the microphone. Her voice is loud and large. Her story is larger.

In the end, she just stepped up to the podium, almost unconsciously put the written script aside, inhaled, and lets it go. She started telling the story straight ahead with clarity and without hesitation, right from her heart—you could hear a pin drop. It was absolutely silent. You could feel her story weighing down on their souls. We were on the sidelines with the CEO of LFY and other main staff. I started just bawling, embarrassed to have them see me crying. Even years later, as I am describing this event, I am crying. Maryam finished. Jennifer and I stepped up on the platform beside our lovely daughter. There we were, in front of the bright lights shining into our eyes. We stepped down and walked to the back of the ballroom, paused some, and walked out of the ballroom into a lobby with couches, sat down, and inhaled. It seemed like such a long walk we were so dazed. Sue and I were emotionally exhausted, but Maryam many-fold more so.

Maryam told us, as she gave the speech, she scanned her eyes across this huge audience and saw a guy fixated on her story. His eyes just locked onto her. At the dramatic moment of the story where Nargiz is choking her, Maryam said that this guy just gasped for air and cried because he was so horrified and shocked. It wasn't just this guy who was moved by the emotion—there wasn't a dry eye in the house.

A well-known NHL hockey player followed Maryam and gave a speech. He was very handsome and had an infectious smile. LFY gave him an award, and he made a short speech. There was more on the agenda, but we were ready to leave. We got into the elevator, and as it turns out, there was this hockey player and his wife. He turned to Maryam and said, "This will not be the last time you tell your story." If I had not cried before, well, I had one more opportunity.

Chapter 3: Neglect and Abuse

Mommy dearest, Shabana, neglects and abuses Maryam

Shabana never held Maryam, never kissed her, never cleaned her hair, never caressed her, never gave Maryam milk from her own breast nor even the milk of human kindness that a child would want and should have from her mother. Shabana never showed love to Maryam in any way, even to this day, and she is thirty-nine years old. Shabana's older sister, the bad aunt, told Shabana she should kill Maryam before or soon after her birth, but even as evil as Shabana is, she couldn't kill her. Shabana neglected and abused Maryam far more than Maryam's two sisters and her brother.

Even Maryam's birth was not easy; She was born a preemie. Shabana and even her doctor did not think she was going to survive past infancy. Shabana did nothing to help her recover. Maryam's skin was splotchy, and she was anemic. As she grew, she became healthy. Her skin became pink and normal, and overall she looked pretty. They ran into the doctor a couple of years later, and he asked, "Who is this?" He was stunned to find out it was Maryam; he really didn't think she would survive. So, even from her birth, Maryam had overcome adversity with her innate resilience.

When Maryam was seven, Shabana beat her unmercifully every which way she could. *At this point, Shabana thought Maryam was dead*!! So she rolled Maryam up in a blanket and took her to a mosque. The imam had unwrapped her, saw she was alive, in pretty bad condition but still alive. Also, he recognized her because he had her in classes teaching the Koran. Her sister Jamila had gone to the mosque to pray, not knowing what had happened with Maryam. She was shocked and took her home to treat her wounds. Amir came home and saw how badly she was beaten and yelled at Jamila for not taking her to the hospital. After calming down, Amir quickly took her to the hospital. Maryam survived this traumatic event, which was just one of a mounting pile of trauma.

When Maryam was eight, Shabana threw a drinking glass at Maryam's face. It shattered in the corner of her left eye socket between the bridge of her nose and the inner end of her eyebrow. Maryam shows us, pointing to the scar nearly twenty years later. Maryam says, "It doesn't really show, so that's why you haven't seen it, and I don't talk about it much." *Shabana threw a drinking glass at her young daughter's face?* This is just so much abuse—the kind of thing in Canada that eventually would lead the Provincial Division of Family and Youth Services to intervene and take the child away from the parents because they are unfit parents.

After Maryam was eleven years old, Shabana made Maryam cook for the family on a regular basis. This could be for another eight or ten family and whoever else was dropping by which might include all her adult siblings, nieces, nephews, aunts, uncles, grandparents, cousins. At times, there could be as many as twenty or thirty people at a meal. She had to cook not just one dish for everyone. She had to cook to order for each one's preferences. It was like running a restaurant, but she was the one cook and one waitress. She would have to get up at 4 am to start cooking and finish up about 8 or 9 pm. Shabana wouldn't let Maryam eat with the family. She had to eat in the kitchen by herself. The physical and verbal abuse and neglect demeaned her self-worth.

While dysfunctional relationships within her family prevailed, they did eat together. Despite the dysfunction, keeping a family together is paramount. I asked Maryam one time, "How does that go when they eat together?" She said, "Oh, yeah, they shout and yell and throw food, and get in fights." I think to myself, "Okay, I got it, I got the picture."

When she was about twelve, Maryam burnt a hot pad. Shabana flipped out and beat her with her hands. Amir came home figured out what was going on, flipped out, and started beating Maryam with a broomstick handle, "...a lot...a lot" Maryam said. "If I had a day I didn't get beaten, it would have been a good day." I tell people these stories, their eyes get so big.

When Maryam was twelve, old enough to figure out this treatment was not normal, she asked her mother, "Why? Why do you treat me like this?" Shabana answered, "It's none of your business". That was the last time Maryam asked. Jamila, Maryam's older sister by eleven years, could see without a doubt that Shabana neglected and abused Maryam far more than her other children. After Maryam came to Canada permanently, Jamila told Maryam she was afraid to ask Shabana why she abused Maryam so much. Jamila just took it as a fact of life. Beyond neglect, Shabana abused her verbally and beat her physically. One time Shabana called Maryam *a bitch*. The river that runs through all this is the mean-spiritedness, the evilness. But Maryam was not able to figure why, why was she singled out? Where was this stuff coming from? There must be some deeper reason.

Another time, it was winter, and the water to clean dishes was cold. Maryam wanted to warm the water to warm her hands. Shabana said, "No, I will put snow and ice in to make the water colder." Shabana takes advantage of every situation that might arise. One time, Shabana beat her with an *electrical cord.*

When Maryam was eleven, Shabana mixed some date rape pills in juice with the intention that it would *render her unconscious so men could rape her without her resisting.* Shabana even charged men to have this sex. This Shabana knows no bounds. The hate in her heart is so vicious, so vile. Maryam would ask herself, "How do I forgive my very own mother, this evil person, for her long litany of neglect, abuse, and atrocities against me?" This is just one more memory that Maryam suppressed and later came out through counseling in Maryam's seventh year with us.

Jamila told Maryam one time, "I was in bed trying to sleep, but I was actually awake, and I heard Mom and Dad arguing with each other more loudly than usual." But this time, she heard Amir say to Shabana, "I think Allah is punishing you for all the terrible things you did to Maryam since before she was born." But Jamila didn't understand what that meant.

Once Maryam asked Amir, "Did my mother ever try to kill me?" He replied, "Well… [stammering around, not wanting to tell the truth] … yes. When you were about eight, she tried to feed you *rat poison.*" Jamila, realizing what Shabana was doing, pulled the glass away from Shabana. If Shabana attempted this one killing, how many other times might she have tried? This isn't the first or last time Jamila saved Maryam.

At age twelve, Maryam took care of her grandmother for several months, and her grandmother gave Maryam a nice dress and shoes as a gift. Maryam was very thankful and treasured it because she had only received hand-me-downs before from her mother, and it wasn't for lack of money. The other kids got new clothes and gifts. But not Maryam.

Shabana came to Maryam and asked, "Where did this come from?"

Her grandmother said, "I gave it to her."

Shabana said, "You don't deserve it. Give that to me!"

Maryam said, "No!"

Shabana grabbed the dress from Maryam and cut it to shreds. Maryam tells us this story ten years after it happened, saying, "This hurt me so bad, worse than even when they beat me." This just tore out her soul. This was just one more way for Shabana to emotionally abuse her daughter.

Years after the so-called marriage with Maryam, Hafiz called Shabana and said he wanted to talk with Maryam because he missed her. At this point, it had been over four years since the marriage she had with Hafiz, which, if you remember, lasted only one week. Can this be? I mean, four years, the guy should just get over it. Maryam said to us, "Hafiz! Who is this guy? He means nothing to me. He is completely in the past; he is out of my mind! I have a life of my own, I have my two Canadian parents, and I make decisions for myself. I surely don't want to talk with him!" Shabana pleaded, "Please talk with him." This shows how manipulative Shabana is. Hafiz is operating from some twisted part of his brain that won't let go of Maryam. If Shabana had her way, she would marry Maryam off to Hafiz *again*, but only for all the money she could get. The bad aunt is many-fold worse and incites Shabana to hurt Maryam as much as possible. Maryam is onto their game. We thought Maryam had matured considerably and moved on emotionally from Hafiz. She was certainly not as crippled by him as she was in the first year with us. She had made a remarkable recovery.

Maryam called home for the first few years with us and spent a lot of time talking with Shabana, and it seemed quite clear that all Maryam wanted was just a little bit of nurturing, care, love… just even the slightest amount. Shabana had cast down so much neglect and abuse on Maryam. Maryam's inner need for love from her mother is understandable. Just a drop of human kindness, the love that only a mother can give, that's all she wanted. As the years have gone by, I think Maryam has honestly started giving up hope for her mother's love. Very gradually over a period of thirteen years, when she lived with her family back in Afghanistan, and twenty-six years with her in our lives, Maryam has let go of her mother emotionally. Ever since day one with Maryam in our lives, I instantly loved her so deeply because I knew Nargiz had almost killed her. But then, as the years have passed, Maryam has told us how much neglect and abuse Shabana had heaped on her, not to mention her dad and the bad aunt. I have just loved Maryam all the more. I think resolving the mountains of emotional trauma through counseling will take the rest of her life.

Amir, does his share

One of the first stories Maryam tells us is about when she first starting to cook for the family. Her father, Amir, didn't like the meal, picked up the plate with the food on it, and threw it against the wall in a fit of anger. After she had started living with us, when I didn't care for a particular dish she had prepared, I would say, "Well, it's not my favorite." Maryam says, "Wow, you're sure not Amir!" I reply, "It's not a difficult thing to do." Amir's behavior was erratic, and it was difficult for Maryam to know which father was going to show up on any given day. One day, Amir gave some money to Jamila to buy some ice cream for Maryam, and the next day, he would beat her. Amir physically abused Maryam a lot, but he mostly treated her nicely and respectfully.

Maryam was eight and when she had gone to her grandfather's house without permission. When she returned, Amir beat her severely and put her in the basement which had absolutely no light. The basement was not completely finished, had moldy air, and lots of garbage—just horrible. Jamila returned to their house and found her there, and got her out. Maryam told us a story when she had been with us six years, she told us one more story of abject abuse. She had suppressed the memory of this event, and it came out during one of her counselling sessions. Maryam said it is so painful to realize one more act of abuse she had suppressed but is glad it is out so she can heal from it. It really seems there is no bottom to the pit of depravity. We continue to ask ourselves, how did this girl survive? Maryam is reciting this story, again without emotion, and in the next breath, she says he was a good man.

At one point, he beat her on the back with a metal pole, another time with an electrical cord. I guess the electrical cords are a weapon of choice, as Shabana used it also.

In Maryam's mind, she feels both the pain of Amir's abuse and, at the same time feels his caring. I find this just baffling, almost like a split personality. On the good side, Amir one time decided that Maryam was the smartest one, and he made sure she went to school starting in the first grade, spending $100 a month on tuition. She did finish high school, which was remarkable in Afghanistan for a girl to finish high school. Contrary to the neglect and abuse Maryam suffered at the hands of her parents and older brother Nargiz, Maryam tells us often how nicely her older sister Jamila treated her.

Amir could be bad sober but worse when drunk, especially when he blacked out and had no idea what he what he had done when he sobered up the next day. When he started drinking, everyone in the family would run into hiding to protect themselves.

Hafiz came to Kunduz before the engagement, and Amir started fully realizing that Maryam was going to get married, that she would move to America, and that he would lose his daughter. He went into a fit of anger and proceeded to physically beat Maryam because she was going to get married even though it was arranged by Shabana! Maryam had nothing to do with making the decision. She was the object of the decision. Don't try to look for logic in this. It all goes back to the underlying theme that the girl is always wrong and needs to be punished. It's embedded in the culture.

The rest of the extended family

Ever since she can remember *Nargiz* had it out for her. Eventually, she found out why he abused her so much—Amir favored her over Nargiz. Wow, that is some case of jealousy. This could play into why he was chosen to do the honor killing also.

Nargiz molested Maryam when she was grade-school age, which would happen when the family was asleep. The family all slept together side-by-side, with Shabana on one end and Amir on the other, making the total as many as 10. For some period, Nargiz and Maryam slept beside each other, and this is when he would molest her. Nargiz told her to be quiet, or he would kill her. He may have meant that figuratively, but later, of course, it was literally. A far less consequential event was the time when Nargiz came back to the house with ice cream for everyone but Maryam. She felt absolutely like a nobody. "It's one thing if I have to cook and clean every day for the whole family, but that really hurt." Being left out of the family group, again and again.

One of the first stories Maryam told us was about the bad aunt was that there was a big gathering of women in the family, even including little girls, something like twenty of them. This is traditional and customary, sitting at one long table, with about ten on each side in this case. The table was set with beautiful food, which Maryam cooked. For the women, it's like a refuge away from men and their abuse. Maryam was twelve and everyone had a seat except her. Even little girls, four- and five-years-old, had seats at the table. Maryam asked the bad aunt where her seat was, to which the bad aunt said, "There is no room at this table for you. You belong in the kitchen. Quit bothering us." Another layer of emotional abuse heaped on the mound covering Maryam. Her aunt continuously cut into Maryam's heart and soul. "I do not think I can ever forget or forgive her for the things she did to me," Maryam said.

The following is an example of how Shabana's mother, Maryam's grandmother, got abused by her very own children, who were middle-age at the time of this event. The abusive nature of Maryam's nuclear family existed within the context of abuse in her extended family. None of Shabana's seven siblings wanted to take care of their mother when she got old and infirm. Eventually, one of the sons, who was extraordinarily rich, reluctantly took her in, but it didn't go well So finally, he kicked his own mother out. Then, some relatives, including Maryam, chipped in to take care of her. They actually paid one relative, not one of the grandmother's children, to take care of her. (Speaking of getting thrown out, Amir got sick one time, and Shabana kicked *him* out of the house and onto the street.) It seems to be a custom in abusive families that when a family member is old or sick or in some way debilitated and weak to, throw them out so they are not a burden. Abuse does not discriminate on the basis of age or status in the house. Abuse is not just for Maryam, but Maryam does get an extra heavy dose.

Nursing her grandfather had some consequences. This particular part of the story starts out good and then, as seems inevitable, goes bad. Maryam's grandfather (Shabana's father) was one hundred and six, and his health started to go down. The dude's a hundred and six, it's gotta happen sooner or later. None of his eight children nor their spouses nor any of the other family members stood up to take care of him. Maryam at age twelve volunteered. Maryam has a huge, loving heart, which is contrary to the heaps of abuse mounded on her. She could have grown up to be a serial killer, and it would be understandable. So Maryam moved into her grandfather's house. Grandfather had been a rich man, He owned many horses (apparently a measure of wealth in earlier generations) and owned many profitable businesses. (Maryam will see some huge building here in Canada getting constructed and jokingly says, "My grandfather is building that!" or "Microsoft, my grandfather owns that!". She really extrapolates and exaggerates and is quite the teller of lengthy fantasy stories. She is quite funny and has a sharp wit.) As his health gradually declined, he told Maryam where a chest was with all of the jewels and money and gave her the key, and told her when he died to take the chest to the imam (a Muslim faith leader) and to tell the imam to give it to the poor. And Maryam pops off, again with her sharp wit, *"Grandfather, I'm poor. Give it to me!"*

Maryam fed him, sometimes soup with a spoon; cleaned him when he soiled his sheets; washed him; she did everything for him. One time, she had fed him and cleaned up and had to go home for something. She returned and everyone, all of the family, were standing around him. She went up to him, felt his forehead, and Maryam told us, "*He was cold!* I was here not too long ago, and he was fine; he was alive." This is one of the first stories Maryam told us, and she repeats it every so often. So it made quite an impression on her. If it is the first person you have seen dead and especially if you are not even a teenager yet, this would be shocking. But in this case, she had a deep emotional attachment to him, *and he treated her kindly*, something Maryam didn't get enough of. Her grandfather had given Maryam a chest full of jewelry and money with its key with instructions that she should take it to the mosque for the imam to distribute to the poor. (An imam is like a priest in the Christian religion).

Her aunts and uncles and her mother knew about the chest and asked her where it was. Maryam said she didn't have it, and they proceeded to—you guessed it—*beat her unmercifully*. And this is a whole group of them, not just one person. It's like a pack of jackals ripping flesh off their prey. Such greed and wanton avarice! They seemed not to miss one form of depravity, and they did it deeply. Finally, they relent. Maryam waits till the dark of night when the coast is clear and spirits the chest, carrying it on her head, to the mosque over several miles. It is large and quite heavy, so it's amazing she made it to give it to the imam. She went out of the house in her bare feet so she wouldn't wake anyone up. By the time she got to the mosque, her feet were raw and bloody.

Yet another story Maryam told us in the first year that Maryam was with us was about *a cousin* who had trouble with her husband, which was so bad *she poured gasoline on herself and set herself on fire.* She died a few days later. It seems to me like the husband didn't directly abuse her with the fire but probably abused her so much that she decided to end it herself. Maryam has told us about other cases of females setting themselves on fire. Domestic violence can happen in any culture, but this is just such a horrific extent. Shocking no matter what.

Random murders in the community took place during the time of Maryam's life. She explained that, "My cousin was murdered." It was like a bombshell going off right next to you. Even though there is this undertow that life is cheap and killing is easy, it's shocking when it happens yet one more time, especially to one close to you. She said it was a cousin on her dad's side (generally the good side vs. Shabana's side). Maryam grew up with him, and they were just about the same age. He visited often and never did anything bad, she tells us. He was Amir's favorite nephew, and Amir, normally not one to show emotion, was upset. The cousin was in Kabul with another family member about his age. Possibly, some small street gang grabbed her cousin and his friend and tortured them. They cut off their fingers and toes and killed them. They wrapped the two of them in plastic, drove them on the six-hour bumpy road to Kunduz, and put them in front of a central mosque. These murderers identified their two victims with information in their phones, which apparently is how they knew they were from Kunduz. It was uncertain if the killers knew their victims. In any case, the father and those in the family who knew what happened decided to keep the information from the mother, at least in the meantime. I asked Maryam if he had lots of brothers, sisters, and cousins. She said, "Oh yeah, dad-jan." ("Jan" is a term of affection which Afghans use frequently.) So much grief.

Other murderers randomly shot dead a twenty-two-year-old cousin for no apparent reason a few blocks from where Amir and Shabana lived. Bad neighborhood or bad country? This adds one more trauma for Maryam, and then the trauma ripples through the family. Maryam also told us about a neighbor when she was about twelve, and she saw commotion down the street. It turns out that some guys kidnapped some young girl, *chopped her up,* and left her body parts back at her parent's house.

This story is about a family in the community that Maryam and her family had known. One evening at dinner, Maryam told us how vicious Amir and Shabana can be with each other. I asked Maryam, is this horridness just them? I told her I think they need a psychiatric exam and treatment. Maryam jumps right back, countering with a story of an Afghan family with four sons and four daughters. They were a wholesome, happy family. Each one was good, and the relationships were healthy. Two of the brothers about the same age had gotten married. The two brothers, who were grown and living out of the house, came home, and their two wives were having a big argument—not just verbally arguing but physically fighting and hitting each other. The brothers tried to stop it and then ended up getting into the fight, hitting each other, and it escalated into a big fist fight amongst the four of them. After everything calmed down, it turned out the reason for the fight was that the one brother bought his wife a fancy gift, and the other wife got so jealous, she physically attacked the other.

The point that Maryam was making was that even the happiest of families sooner or later will have a son marry someone who is dysfunctional and sort of "infect" the happy family, turning it into an unhappy, dysfunctional family which in turn spreads into Afghan society. It takes only a little infection to spread if not cured. Because the larger Afghan society is so depraved, the chances of one being infected are high. If Afghanistan was not suffering from such depravity, I think that the chances of a healthier society would prevail. With the Taliban taking over, it makes the situation all the more problematic—just more implosion of the society. Then there is the fundamental behavior that stems back millennia through tribal mores.

Maryam's life compared my life

I listen to these stories Maryam tells, and I am aghast. I am seventy-seven years old and this is true for my life as an adult. However, when I was growing up in Pennsylvania, I did have some life experience that was closer to Maryam's stories. I went to a grade school that had kids from working class to abjectly poor families many from the West Virginia part of Appalachia. I was in the seventh grade, and this sixteen-year-old boy got a girl in my class pregnant at age thirteen. A year later, the baby was crying, so he shot the mother. They were from the poorest part of the poor part of town. Even back at the time when I was thirteen, I knew this sixteen-year-old kid was frustrated and angry about life in general. He was known as a bully in the neighborhood. He barely had the ability to take care of himself let alone a thirteen-year-old wife and a baby, which shaped his behavior. I imagine he felt desperate about what to do, where to go and took it out by shooting the mother of his child.

My high school had 2,000 students, fifty percent white and fifty percent black, mostly working class to poor. My freshman year had six hundred students, and my graduating class had under three hundred, yielding an over a fifty percent dropout rate. A lot of students became unwed teen mothers and were part of that fu percent dropped out. The high school building was like a massive fortress with a total of 2,000 students. Poor white and black kids went out to the back side of the building to the poor neighborhoods, and there was a lot of fighting going on. The better-off kids went out the front, where social action was guys and girls talking. After graduation, some of our classmates, most often poor, often black, fell fatal victims to gun violence even within the first couple of years.

About sixty of my graduating class were in college prep classes. Almost all started to college and about fifty finished college. We, as a group, were motivated to move up from those poorer beginnings. We were driven to have a better life, and we did. We wanted to move up the income and sociocultural ladder. The worst part of what we were getting away was poverty-based violence. I didn't experience that in my family, but it was happening all around me. So, my perspective changed in the sixty years since then. Even then, my experiences when I was young do not compare to the tribal vendettas and viciousness of violence in Afghanistan.

When I hear Maryam's stories, I'm shocked. Most of the people I tell her stories to are as aghast as I am. But they are from the same sociocultural status as I am. My perceptions of "Canadian society" is a sweeping generalization that encompasses many, many sub-cultures. Bad things happen in Canada. In my life experience, domestic violence, homicide, suicide, and the like are rare. But then I, my family, and friends are primarily white, middle class, middle-aged, well educated, and financially secure. Others, who didn't have those advantages, would have more difficulty being financially secure by definition. I believe poorer families have higher frequencies of domestic violence and social dysfunction. By definition, poorer people have more stress just making a living. They are closer to an emotional edge, which can take only a little bit of challenge to push a family into abuse and even violence.

"…Being poor further entraps the survivor in the abuse and often lengthens any process she may go through to escape—as well lengthens entrapment in poverty. The intersection of poverty and domestic violence further endangers survivors, their children, and our communities as a whole."[1]

This is Canada which has its share of poverty, but then there is Afghanistan which has a substantial poverty. The fertility rate for Canada in 2020 was 1.40^2 , and the fertility rate for Afghanistan in 2022 was 3.99 births per woman[3] making Afghanistan have a fertility rate 2.85 times higher than Canada. This is a striking demographic difference.

There is a correlation of wealth, and in a recent study, socioeconomic status was found to have a definite influence on birth and death rates, with higher socioeconomic status resulting in lower birth and death rates. This effect was independent of such confounding variables as the age structure of the population, religion, and region.[4]

Afghanistan is after all a third-world country. According to Maryam, in her Afghan family, there are parents, children, grandchildren tied together tightly, sharing meals, visiting with each other often (weekly or daily). It's a real ebb and flow of families connecting continuously, which is what I call the spaghetti bowl. So when there's a dysfunctional Afghan family, the family is much larger and more tightly connected than in Canada for the most part. The dysfunction can easily spread through the extended family. However, the term "dysfunction" does not capture some of the ghastly behaviors that I describe in this book, reflecting the appalling depth of depravity. In Canada, we have domestic violence, but in Afghanistan, it is more vicious, in my opinion.

Reaction of friends

Most of my friends are aghast when I tell them some of the horror stories—to a person. But then my friends are primarily white, middle class, middle aged, well educated, and financially secure—like me. Some friends I told the story to reacted impassively, showing no emotion. I interpreted that as just emotionally shielding off the horror. Another time, I told a friend some things about Shabana. Her response was that Maryam should dump her mother because she has done no good to her, which is the same feeling we have had. But we know how hard it has been for Maryam to let go of her mother. There is nothing stronger than a child wanting the love of her mother, and in the case of Shabana, even after all the things she has done to Maryam. Four years after Maryam entered our lives, I was visiting an old friend and his wife, whom I hadn't seen for a long time. We reminisced and talked about all kinds of things. Then I told them the Maryam story. I got to the honor killing and found myself crying—once again, I thought I was over that. They were compassionate and patted me on my shoulder, saying, "It's okay, it's okay."

I told an African-Canadian friend a short version of the Maryam story, the honor killing, and us taking her in. My friend said yes, she knows about these things. They found out about a father in Senegal who was going to sell off his one daughter. My friend and her husband extracted the girl from Senegal and adopted her. It turned out that that girl had a sister whose father was going to sell her off, too. My friend and her husband extracted the sister and adopted her too. This friend is the only one I've run into who has such a story comparable to ours.

Revelations thirty nine years later

It was 2021 , Maryam got a call from her sister Jamila, who gave her some information stemming back to her birth. *Shabana was raped, and Maryam was the child born out of this rape. This is the root of all the abuse!!* Now she really knows why Shabana has abused her so badly! Shabana didn't have to abuse her, but she did. At least, it is plausible. Her older sister and brother, Jamila and Nargiz, and her father, Amir, knew back at the time it happened. Only Maryam was never told. This would explain a lot about why Shabana abused, neglected, punished, beat, and attempted to kill this little girl. Maryam can remember Shabana treating her this way since her earliest memories. Maryam always told us that Amir had abused her a lot, but on the other hand, at times he was kind and loving to her. Maryam bent her head and said, "Yes, he loved me if he would stay with Shabana and take care of me, and he was not even my birth father."

Now, there is one more event, one more step into the deep, dark past yet to be revealed. Several months after Jamila's revelation, Shabana had a major health scare, and she seemed to have a self-reckoning, like, "I better tell the whole truth before I die or I'll go to hell." (She'd have to do a heck of a lot more than one story to keep from going to hell!!) This is a very crucial piece of Shabana and Maryam's history, and she revealed it to Maryam so many years after the fact. It goes like this. When Maryam was born, *Shabana and her rapist*

CONSPIRED to marry Maryam off to Hafiz, who, get this, *is the son of the rapist.*

This makes Hafiz and Maryam half-brother and half-sister, which would furthermore drain the gene pool to a lower level. The rapist is a cousin of Shabana, *also making Hafiz and Maryam second cousins <u>and</u> half-brother and half-sister!!* When Jennifer and I first heard about the tight family relations, we wondered about the diversity of the gene pool, having seen Hafiz's deformed arms. It's a wonder Maryam was not deformed in some way. The rest of the conspiracy is that Shabana and the rapist instructed Hafiz to declare Maryam not a virgin, to stay married for one week and then send her back to Afghanistan, so that Maryam would be seen as dishonoring the family! Shabana knew that Maryam was not a virgin because Maryam had been raped previously, but that is a story for another chapter.

As part of this elaborate plot, Shabana and the rapist *instructed Nargiz* to regain the family honor, following ancient tradition. Jennifer, Maryam, and I knew the attempted honor killing had happened but didn't know *why* until six years later. We thought there was some reason, but what was it? We didn't know that Shabana and the rapist conspired to commit a premeditated murder, a plot to kill Maryam. This was not just an arranged marriage but an *arranged honor killing!* When Nargiz was choking Maryam, Shabana yelled, "Kill her, kill her"—this was all pre-meditated, all according to the script. *Killing Maryam would regain the honor lost because of Shabana's rape.* Shabana knew that Maryam was not a virgin, thus making it a premeditated loss of honor. Then, the angel intervened and rescued Maryam and sent her off to Kabul. Of course, Maryam was very disturbed to hear the *whole story.* This would seem to be the last piece of the puzzle to explain why Shabana abused Maryam throughout all of her years. In any case, what a tangled web they wove.

All of these stories tell me a woman's right to freedom from violence should be a human right.

Chapter 4: How Many Times Can a Girl Get Raped?

Suppressed memory

One of Maryam's counselors applied the EMDR method, a psychotherapy treatment that was originally designed to alleviate the distress associated with traumatic memories. EMDR stands for Eye Movement Desensitization and Reprocessing, a mouthful but very effective. For Maryam, it brought about an astounding breakthrough, bringing out a deeply seated, suppressed memory. Maryam had blanked out some very dramatic events, equal to the horrific attempted honor killing. Maryam pulled out from her deep memory that *she had been raped several times before the marriage* with Hafiz. This explains that she really was not a virgin as Hafiz claimed and as Maryam denied—Maryam just didn't know. This makes sense. If she had suppressed the memory of these rapes, she wouldn't remember she had sex at all.

Maryam was about twelve when the bad cousin Rakhman raped her. He is the son of the bad aunt. When she was ten, Nargiz raped her. When she was six, the bad cousin Rakhman raped her for the first time. I am telling you, *Maryam got raped when she was six years old!* This is just beyond my ability to comprehend. Maryam says the bad cousin took her into the bathroom in their house and she exclaims, *"Then there was blood on the floor!!"* At the time, she really didn't know what this was all about—the concept of "rape" was just not in the realm of her understanding. It was just so traumatic, her mind suppressed it, which must have been an involuntary coping mechanism.

When this was revealed in her counseling session, Maryam immediately called Shabana. It so happened Shabana was with all the women in the family: grandma, Jamila, Siddiqa (wife of Nargiz), and other women and older girls. The phone was at grandma's house, and the speaker was on. Shabana said she didn't want to talk about it. Grandma countered Shabana's attempt to delay the truth yet another time. Grandma said, "It's time to talk about this." Maryam recited the series of rapes going back to age six. Grandma said to Maryam, "If we had told you what was going on at the time of any one of these rapes, we were afraid you would commit suicide." Maryam was, of course, furious at finding out about this string of horrific events. This explained a lot, and it was one more serious, important part of Maryam's mountain of trauma that was brought out. It's like lancing a boil and letting the puss come out so then the skin, body, and mind could heal.

Grandma further revealed that the bad aunt, the mother of the bad cousin who raped Maryam at age six, did not want Maryam's rape to dishonor *her* family. Therefore, to regain *her* family's honor, the bad aunt told her sister Shabana, *"Kill Maryam, kill the bastard."* This was *a little girl.* She's only six years old and you want to kill her to regain *your* family's honor?? Contrary to other times Shabana tried to kill Maryam, Shabana replied she just couldn't kill Maryam. The bad aunt then said, *"Well, if you're not going to kill her, abuse her enough that she will commit suicide."* This revelation, going down to the time Maryam was six years old, did not come till Maryam was twenty or fourteen years after the event. Shabana, even to this day, still abuses Maryam in every way she can. But Maryam has survived it all with a most remarkable resilience. This is another story illustrating the depth of the roots of this evilness.

Maryam explained that when she was five, the Taliban was bombing in her neighborhood. Amir took his family, a total of eight, down to the basement. The Taliban bombed their house and disintegrated it, but the family survived with only a few injuries. At this point, they moved into the bad aunt's house. Once there, the bad cousin had opportunity to rape Maryam. Maryam had told us about the Taliban bombing their house early on in her years with us. It was a prominent memory even though she was only five years old when it happened. But this is understandable—getting bombed is a pretty significant event. The rape, which happened within a year after the bombing, was significant too, but so traumatic it got suppressed.

Well... just one more rape

Maryam started dating this Afghan-Canadian guy who turned out to be a horror all on his own. He managed to import the worst parts of Afghan culture to Canada all by himself. This event took place the second year after Maryam moved in with us. Jennifer and I felt this relationship was not good. We started to set some boundaries, like when to be back home at night, where she was going to be, and who she was going to be with. The first morning after I had this talk with her about this, I was doing work at my desk, and she came down the stairs and stood right in front of me with her hands on her hips and said defiantly and emphatically, "Dad, *I can't follow these rules*. It's just too much. I need to live my own life." I could have said, "If you want to live your own life, you can find another house to live in." But I didn't say that. She really would not make it on her own. We needed to guide her to a better path.

Because of the issues with this Afghan-Canadian guy, we got her into counseling. He was the right kind of counselor. He was sixty-something and had extensive experience with adolescents and young adults. The first session was to be with the three of us. After a few minutes, Maryam sent us out of the room so she could talk to him alone. After the session, we found out that she said to the counselor, repeating her attitude about this, "I don't need counseling. They are trying to set boundaries for me. I don't need boundaries, and I just can't live with them." After that, we had a few sessions with the three of us, focusing on her relationship with this guy. Maryam said he was "a good guy." When Maryam met anyone, she would identify them as good or bad, no shades in between. Maryam said, "He treats me nicely, but more importantly, he loves me."

The counselor explained she needed to think about it this way. Say this wall is the big picture, but you have your face up against the wall so closely, you can see only a little bit of the wall; you can't see the whole wall, which is the big picture. The whole wall is going to show you more things, and they are different things, maybe some good things and maybe some bad things. Another point he made was that in his many years of counseling he found that a new couple is usually on their best behavior in the beginning. But, within eleven months they will reveal their true behavior. I found it interesting that this apparently was so scientific that it was eleven months, not ten or twelve. And the real behavior may turn out to be some good things, but it may be some things that are not so pleasant. Maryam remained completely unconvinced. She was in love. We only got a few sessions in for Maryam. We should have stayed focused and continued with the counseling because she really needed it. But this counselor retired, and it took a while till we started with another counselor.

Originally, Maryam told us she had met him at school. The truth was that unbeknownst to Jennifer and me, Maryam went on Facebook to look for a guy, someone to date. From day one with us, we told her *not* to get on Facebook. At that time, our purpose was that we didn't want Nargiz to worm his way into our house and finish off the honor killing. The honor killing story is scary, and it scared us. Also, Facebook, in general, could end up giving you real-life problems you don't want. But we couldn't control her every move. We learned that people, institutions, etc., set up rules to guide some behavior, but then people break those rules. Sure enough, Maryam was ready to break the rules like any unruly teenager is bound to do. Then there is the Afghan element which is that as a young girl in Afghanistan lives life that is very constrained compared to western countries for the most part. Once in Canada, Maryam had a lot of freedom every which way. We had had two kids before, but they had no issues, and they were grown adults and out of the house by the time Maryam showed up. So Maryam's issues were all new and took some adjusting for us. But within a year after she had moved in with us, she found this guy on Facebook.

We noticed some weird stuff about her coming and going for a few months. She often would say her ride was going to pick her up down the block. Then she caved and decided to introduce us, albeit in a very awkward way. Jennifer, Maryam, our next-door neighbor, and I were going to a restaurant. On the way down, she was on the phone talking in the Farsi language. (It was and is very common for her to do this in front of us, which we told her was rude but to no avail. However, this practice is very common among the younger generation in general.) She said that somebody was going to meet her, but we didn't understand really what she was saying. We went into the restaurant and were about halfway through our meal when this guy came in and stood in front of us at our table, not saying anything. He looked like he could be an Afghan. We looked over at Maryam, and she was looking at the wall opposite him and practically slunk completely under the table. Finally, after this very long, awkward spell, he introduced himself as Maryam's "boyfriend." This is the first time we have heard about a *boyfriend.*

Jennifer has a very keen sense of who might be a good guy or a bad guy. It's like antennae with lasers that hone in on danger. Jennifer's hackles really straight up on her back upon meeting this "boyfriend." After talking briefly, he left, and we finished dinner. We got into the car, and Maryam told us to go to another place, and it turns out that she jumped out of our car and into his car without saying goodbye. It began a relationship that would last for nearly a year. It was as if she was under an evil spell that got worse and worse. I am just the opposite of Jennifer. When I meet someone new I just think they are a good person—give them all the credit until proven otherwise. This guy's name is Ghulam, and he is Afghan-Canadian. I wanted to make peace between Jennifer and him, so I invited him to dinner with us at a restaurant. By the time dinner was over, he still seemed OK to me, but Jennifer continued to be very troubled by him. One time, I asked him where he worked, and he said he worked for Lowes Hardware. He was rather vague—a red flag.

This relationship went on for some time, then the bottom fell out. Jennifer got up in the middle of the night and heard some noise in Maryam's room. She went over and opened the door. *There is Ghulam and Maryam—having sex!* He pulled his clothes on and ran out of the house. Jennifer didn't tell me until morning when I'm getting up. I said, *"WHAT??!!"* I marched over to Maryam's room and started yelling at her with every swear word I knew. I was enormously angry. Up to this point, I was never angry with her. I always treated her with respect. Not this time. I told her that she had better start packing her bags because I was kicking her out of the house. I went to work and simmered all day, putting it in the back of my head but not resolving it at all. I came to the end of the workday, and I thought, "I am going to kick her out!" I was still very angry when I got home and told Jennifer where I was at on the situation, and she said, *"You can't kick her out! She has no place to go."* I came to realize Jennifer was right, I couldn't kick her out. I went up to Maryam's room, and there she was with many bags packed and garbage bags full of her belongings, sitting sullen and dejected.

I asked, "What are you going to do. *This guy is not going to take you in, is he?"*

"No, Dad, no he's not."

In this period in the fall, Maryam said that he never took her to where he lived. Ghulam had told her he was splitting the rent with some guy who wanted his privacy. To us, this sounded suspicious, that he was hiding something. Much later, it turned out he was living with some woman. Also, he did not show up in person at our house after the "incident," and she was gone a lot. She was continuing to walk down the street far enough we couldn't see his car. They were on the phone a lot, but we couldn't tell if it was him or somebody else speaking Farsi. Time and again we would try to tell her this guy was no good. Some of our friends tried to tell her the same thing, but to no avail.

Maryam told her family in Kunduz what was happening with this new guy. They told her to drop the guy. Maryam didn't want to take any advice. She felt she was in love, and that was that. He had such control of her emotions she couldn't let go.

My theory about this is she is a victim in the way of the battered-woman syndrome. Nargiz certainly beat her. Shabana neglected her, physically beat her, and emotionally abused her. Amir beat her. Emotional neglect (not touching her tenderly or paying any kind of loving attention) can be worse than emotionally or physically beating someone, I think. The bad aunt abused her also. Then there were the many rapes. All this left her with monstrous PTSD. So, I think all this neglect and beating shaped Maryam's frame of emotional reference. Getting beaten was just the way life was. She was a perfect candidate for falling into the battered wife syndrome—find a new boyfriend, and if he's abusive, he is a perfectly treacherous fit. Maryam had learned amazing coping skills, but not far beneath is a huge layer of neglect and abuse.

This left Maryam extremely vulnerable to anyone coming along and doing the same. She didn't know anything different. Jennifer and I found out later that Ghulam trolled the college campus, restaurants, bars, and other places where young, vulnerable Afghan-Canadian girls hung out. He had radar for these girls. He was not looking for a long-term mate. He was looking for some girl first to abuse and then second to have sex with. It didn't hurt that he had a nice car to help prey on the vulnerable. I have heard professionals in the field say that a rapist's motivation is more about control than sex, and Ghulam had strong emotional control over Maryam. He was the master, and she was the petulant slave, sniveling for any morsel of attention, which sadly included him beating her. She struggled valiantly to let go. She would go back and forth.

Maryam grew more distant from us. She was old enough to get herself into a mess but not mature enough to take care of herself emotionally. After about his fifth month with Maryam, he told her that he was taking tests to work as a translator for the Canadian equivalent of the CIA in Afghanistan. I think, now, if I was applying for a job with such an agency, I wouldn't say that to anyone. So it came to a certain day in November that he told her he was going to leave the country. By this time, we had come not to trust anything he said. Maryam was getting more and more anxious because she didn't want to see him go. She was in love. She called him on what he said was his last night before going to Afghanistan, and he was at some party, drinking it up. She was so hurt that he hadn't chosen to spend that time with her; she was just devastated.

Time passed, and he had been gone for about six months, and she really was on sharp, tender hooks. About this time, she was hearing that he would be back in Toronto in a few more months. Again, we never trusted what he said about anything, including his whereabouts. As the days went by Maryam became more and more fearful and extremely nervous. She was so afraid this guy would show up at any place she might be. She really did not want to see him. She worked at a retail store. One of her co-workers told Ghulam where she was working.

Maryam had been dating a *nice* Afghan-Canadian Mohammad, her age and just the opposite manner from Ghulam. Mohammad was just the gentleman, something Maryam really needed. Fearing Ghulam, Maryam decided to move away from our house because Ghulam knew where our house was. She found an apartment halfway between our house and Mohammad's apartment, where he lived with his family. This apartment building had a hundred some units, and you had to make an application. We cosigned for financial backing and shelled out the first and last month's rent, $2,000. Mohammad helped her pack up her belongings. She and Mohammad got halfway down the road to the new apartment. She had white knuckles, and then her feet went cold. She just couldn't do it—all of her blood was going to her heart to protect her from the threat in a fight or flight moment. She said to Mohammad, "Turn around." She was so torn—fearful of Ghulam showing up at the store and maybe at our place, but not ready to live in an apartment on her own in a large apartment building where some rapist might be lurking down the hall or around the corner in an unfamiliar neighborhood. At least we provided a degree of security, and she knew the neighborhood. She was so anxious and fearful, it was just palpable. Finally, he showed up at the store.

He begged her, "Please come back, please come back to me. *I love you so much.*"

She said, "You are disrupting business. This is where I am working; you are pathetic—*go away!*"

He pleaded, "Please come back. I am a changed man. I will treat her nicely. *I will treat you like the princess that you are!!*"

The next moment, he would rage at her abusively and would demean her.

"How could I have even looked at you? You are so ugly. You are worthless and stupid. You can't even read. I have met your family in Afghanistan, and they are all worthless and stupid. You are just a little girl, like a little baby rat. *You are a fucking, ugly bitch, a cunt, a fucking whore!*"

He kept going back and forth, pleading for her to come back to him and, in the next breath, berating her in the most vile way. Maryam was enormously embarrassed. Her co-workers and customers were shocked. This was all out in the middle concourse of a sizeable mall. It was essentially in the public square. Over the next month, he showed up at the store several times, would find her other places, and calls her on the phone, going back and forth between pleading and berating. Finally, he prevailed, lured her into his car—like a moth drawn to the fatal attraction of the flame—and drove her to a hotel.

Maryam screamed, "*What's going on?!*" He lured her into the hotel and said, "I just want to be close to you." He pulled her dress up and her panties down. Maryam said afterward, "He forced his way into me." When he was done, he sneered, "*You fucking no good bitch.*" He dropped her off at a location that wasn't easy for her to get back to the store or home—he abandoned her. She was in shock, faint and dizzy. She couldn't believe what she had allowed him to do.

Maryam didn't tell us about the rape until about a week later. The question was whether to tell the police or not. She was hesitant, even reluctant. I thought to myself, we know for sure she had a lot of sex with this bastard, so he could easily say it was consensual. But then I saw how traumatized she was. Maryam has lied to us very convincingly before, but this time, we were quite sure that she was telling the truth. In any case, from that time forward Maryam, Jennifer, and I referred to him as the "rape guy" never by his name, again depersonalizing the rape guy. But even more, we did our best to not discuss the event any more than we had to. It's like a mass shooting. The people most closely involved don't want the perpetrator to have an identity or public recognition. The media has been increasingly taken toward respecting victims by focusing on the event, not the perpetrator. This was Maryam's way to depersonalize him, to work on preventing her mind from bringing up an image of the rape guy.

As with Hafiz, Maryam was concerned that she could suffer if she filed legal charges. There could be direct harm, or somehow, through the strands of the spaghetti bowl, there could be indirect repercussions even for her family back home. Even in Canada it is difficult for a woman to prevail on a rape charge. At a minimum, she would have to relive the rape and deepen the trauma. Having to speak in public before an open court, and telling the most horrible details might be just too much. Despite the downsides, she finally decided to do it. We called the local police. An older policeman and a younger one came. The younger one did the questioning, and while he appeared to be very new, he was very empathetic, very gentle, asking questions step by step leading Maryam to describe what happened, the events leading up to the rape. We thought the younger policeman was a better choice than the older one; the older one seemed jaded and not empathetic. Painfully, she explained from the beginning at the mall, getting into his car, into the hotel, down to the final, "and he put himself in me." How difficult to say that again and conjure up the mental image, the trauma.

She could remember enough about the hotel that the sheriff could find it, another piece of corroboration. We never heard that the police went to the hotel to see any record of him registering, credit card, video tapes that would have given more certain information that they were there and on a certain day, information that would have given context. Even with the context, it would still come to a he-said-she-said situation. At least the name of the rape guy would go into the sheriff's report, and should another girl accuse this guy of rape again, the sheriff could see a pattern.

The sheriff connected her with a case worker who was to handle her case. Maryam decided to file for a restraining order. Jennifer took Maryam to court to get a restraining order. If he violated it, he would get into some sort of punishment and perhaps lead to a mark on his record should he rape again. The police could not find an address for him, and we didn't have enough numbers and letters on his license plate to track him down that way. Thus, they could not serve him with the restraining order. The rape guy had told Maryam he would be out of the country, but we were never sure whether he was telling the truth or lying. The sheriff put his name on a watch list with the sheriff's office and other authorities. If he was out of the country and reentering Canada, he could be apprehended at the border, brought before the court, and served with the order. While court was not able to "serve the warrant" the order existed in the court records.

The order was effective for six months, and if, at the end of the six months, Maryam wanted to extend it, the court would allow another two years. At the end of the six months, Jennifer took Maryam back to the court. Jennifer, Maryam, and I thought this would be perfunctory and, therefore, that we would not need a lawyer. We had nothing prepared to make a clear statement defending Maryam's case. We had heard nothing about him for over a half a year, so we had no reason to think the rape guy would show up. Jennifer and Maryam walked in, looked over the courtroom, and *there he was,* the rape guy with his lawyer, Nazifa, and Hanifa—Maryam's erstwhile "friends". *And he was drunk.* His lawyer asserted that the accusation about the rape was false because he wasn't in the country then. Siddiqa and Hanifa testified to support that fact.

The rape guy, his lawyer, Siddiqa, and Hanifa PURGERED themselves.

It was as if the rape guy had these two girls under his spell, under his control. Jennifer and I, let alone Maryam, had little experience with lawyers and the courtroom. We were learning the hard way that jurisprudence is not necessarily fair or supported by the truth. Maryam and Jennifer were in shock and disbelief, I mean a lot of shock and disbelief. The rules of the court were that Jennifer couldn't speak unless Maryam asked her to. Maryam was in such shock she could hardly speak at all. Jennifer could have explained things to make some sort of case for Maryam. In short order, the judge dismissed the case, and they all walked out. Jennifer and Maryam waited until the rape guy and his entourage left. Maryam could not stand getting an inch closer to him than she had to. When they came home and told me what had happened, they were still in shock and very disturbed. Even now, a couple of years later, the shock and trauma of the whole courtroom scene replays in her mind and gut. All of it was horrific, but Siddiqa standing there, outright lying to protect the slime ball, that was especially painful. Siddiqa had been one of her closest friends, she had been to our house several times, they had spent lots of time together. The common bond was coming to Canada about the same time, learning English as a second language, acculturating to a new way of life, different food, and so many other things like this. And now, Siddiqa turned on Maryam and *stabbed Maryam in the back.* This really hurt Maryam. Maryam had worked with Hanifa, and she had actually asked Maryam to live with her. The picture is seared on her memory—one more layer of trauma on top of the mountain of PTSD already there.

Maryam had a regularly scheduled counseling session after that. Maryam felt guilty, that it was all her fault, and that she was weak. Her counselor said,

"Look at the situation this way. You were strong enough to file the report, strong enough to bring a restraining order for six months, strong enough to go to court to request an extension to two years. He was the weak one, *the* one who got a lawyer to defend him and even felt compelled to lie to the attorney. And he was the one to get Siddiqa and Hanifa to come, get them to lie for him, and to get them to stab you in the back. *Maryam, you are the strong one here. He is weak one.*"

A year or so after the rape guy was no longer on the scene, Maryam told us some of what actually happened, that he was smoking, messing with other women, drinking, and other things we know she abhors. But he ensnared her. Again, this all fits into the battered wife syndrome. He was even drinking and driving to the point of being in very dangerous situations and nearly having accidents. She kept on letting him drive. He was also beating her. We didn't see bruise marks, but she said that when he beat her, that she covered up the bruises so that we wouldn't see them. Why did all this abuse happen to her again? We think it is because she had experienced so much abuse it was the only thing she knew. We know not all Afghan men are this way, but it seems to me a way higher percentage happens in Afghanistan than in Canada. Maryam alone had so many Afghan men beating and otherwise abusing her, plus all the stories of other Afghan girls getting beat up and worse. Degradation seemed to be normal. Maryam suffering at the hands of Afghan men was dramatic.

It's just scary that see all of this tragedy with our own eyes happen to Maryam, it just rips our hearts out. We tell friends, and their jaws drop, or they just get a blank look on their face, like they don't want to think that such horror is going on in this world.

This story demonstrates how some Afghan men, and in a scary way, some Afghan women, have migrated to Canada carrying some of the most horrible parts of Afghan behavior, and never missed a beat—it's all intact. And Maryam has continued to suffer from it. The spaghetti bowl keeps sliding around, oozing back and forth, the good and the bad. Toronto, where we lived, had a large population of Afghan-Canadians, so it was like a "little Kabul", a critical mass of Afghan society, enough strands of noodles to have its own spaghetti bowl and nasty parts of it.

Chapter 5: Family, Girlfriends, and Boyfriends

This is the family and friends of Maryam Najibullah, who was thirteen in 1995 the year this story starts.

Shabana, the mother

Shabana is the most problematic person in Maryam's life. I write fully about her in the chapters about the honor killing and neglect and abuse.

Amir, the father

For a period of several years, Amir made $500 a month working for the United Nations distributing mosquito netting and other humanitarian goods, but then that program came to an end. When he earned that money, he was able to provide well for his family and not have the stress of poverty. He managed to save $15,000 but then spent it all on Nargiz and Parwana's wedding. I exclaimed to Maryam, "He could have saved that for his retirement!" she replied, "Yah, you're right dad." At some point soon after that, he endured some sort of physical disability, which made it more difficult for him to find work. At one point, he found a job as a night watchman. He earned his first paycheck, and some hoodlums accosted him and stole the paycheck. It seems there's guys trolling the streets of Afghanistan, just ready to pounce on somebody with a few bucks. Dejected, Amir gave up the job. I'm not really sure why

Amir hasn't worked since then for so many years. He just seems to have lost his motivation to work and to provide for his family, who for many years in the time of this book included Shabana, Jamila, Nargiz, and Maryam.

Jamila

Jamila is the oldest of Maryam's siblings. She married Sayeed, and they have Abdullah and Laila, who are seven and four in 2000. Jamila was always the most quiet and meek, never one to be pushy. She sometimes didn't take care of her health because she didn't want to be a financial burden on the family. She didn't have good dental hygiene and ended up having most of her teeth pulled out, costing the family much more than if she had taken care of her teeth in the first place.

Abdullah is very tender and loving, but from the time he started talking he started speaking and acting like an adult. He expressed his strong opinion about matters of morals, right and wrong, what people should be doing, finances, you name it. One time, Shabana gave him a bike, but he refused to accept it because he told her she was very wrong to try to sell off Maryam in the arranged marriage.

Nargiz

Nargiz of course, fits most prominently in this story as the one who attempted the honor killing of Maryam. He is the second oldest and has two kids, and beats his wife constantly, following the example of his parents. His wife is Parwana, who is backbiting and arrogant. They lived with Amir and Shabana early in their marriage, and he didn't pay for housing or food at all. For some time, he didn't have a job at a time when there were jobs to be had. Finally, he did get a job, moved his family out, and then at least wasn't mooching off his parents, but didn't help them either. As the years have gone by, he seems to have grown out of his aggressive nature and become a little more socially acceptable. He even asked Maryam to be forgiven for his attempt at the honor killing, but Maryam doesn't trust it. In my mind, it would take a long time to gain trust after someone tried to kill me.

Sayeed

Sayeed married Jamila. He has given himself selflessly to the most vulnerable in the family. He protected Maryam in a dark and scary hotel from the threat of death by her brother Nargiz. Sayeed filled that dark place with his love and his light and then got the plane ticket for Maryam to fly to Canada.

Cousins

One of the first things Maryam told us was that she had a hundred and forty cousins. We found out that she keeps in close touch with seemingly most of them and knows what's happening with whom, who is getting married, who had a child, who got divorced, who had a fight, just daily events. Also, the number of cousins keeps rising due to births. Another thing though, is that she will be talking about so-in-so cousin, only to find out later that they were a just a good friend whom they call cousins. Even a casual acquaintance can quickly become a "cousin." One time, she was on an eight-way FaceTime with eight cousins in eight countries. Distance does not interfere with keeping family relations tight.

Girlfriends

One underlying thrust of this book is that males abuse females at a horrendous rate in Afghanistan and Canada. What about the flip side? If women and girls are getting so much abuse, where do they have to turn to let out their frustration and anger? My theory is that some girls take out their frustrations about males abusing them on other girls. The following stories include some about Maryam's girlfriends, who are all about Maryam's age.

The first step in Maryam meeting a new girlfriend is the utterance of the first word in the Dari dialect of Farsi—then they knew they had a fellow Afghan. Speaking their native tongue is a lot easier than the second language. That is the steppingstone into the shared culture, which was more comfortable than this "Canadian" culture they were immersed in. A girlfriend would be good in the beginning, but then the girlfriend would get so preoccupied with her own problems she would unload them on Maryam. Sharing feelings is fine and natural enough, but when the friend's burden would get to be too heavy, then we would tell Maryam it might be time to move away from that friend. Maryam would quickly agree. I theorize that some Afghan girls have lots of problems; they don't have many friends, and all but pounce on anyone near that is open to being a friend. If they have problems, then they have something in common with Maryam and that tightens the bond. But then all too quickly, the bonds are broken.

Maryam met a new friend, Sakina, at the community college where Maryam took English as a second language (ESL), close to where we lived. This one day, Maryam went to the bathroom at school, said "hello", and heard a Farsi accent replying, and the two fell into intense conversation in Farsi. (The joke became that she met all of her Afghan girlfriends in the bathroom.) We came to pick Maryam up, and she and this new friend had been fully engaged in conversation for over an hour. Sakina gave us a brief account of her situation. She came to Canada when she was twelve to live with her uncle, who provided housing and food but is not kind or attentive and is at times, verbally abusive. Jennifer and I have a soft part in our hearts for such a young girl in need. We impulsively say, "You can stay with us." She says, "No, no, it's okay; I've learned to cope with it." Afghan girls abuse one another—another thread in the dark social fabric of Afghanistan.

Sakina was about twenty-one and finishing up courses at NOVA and had some credits toward a four-year degree. She is exotically attractive in an Afghan sort of way and works and works as a *maître d'* at the Ritz Carlton restaurant in downtown Toronto—not a bad gig. Before, she worked at Victoria's Secret at a mall, which I think sort of reflects her mindset of looking sexy.

She lived about an hour away from our place, depending on traffic, so we figure it'll be a stretch for her to come visit, but she does have her own car. Early on, they were driving around, and a cop pulls her over for speeding. She sweet talks him, and she gets out of the ticket. Not too long later, they're driving around on her own, and she rear-ends a guy, and they both get moderate whiplash. This Sakina is not a good driver.

Sure enough, not long later, she was out driving on her own, got in a wreck, and landed in the hospital. She called Maryam and her brother. Jennifer, Maryam, and I quickly drove down to the hospital, and she was pretty banged up. Even after not having a car, she would take the mass transit to the station nearest us, and then we'd go pick her up, or she'd take Uber.

When Sakina and Maryam would get together, they would go up in Maryam's room and do I don't know what and then would come downstairs laughing and giggling. Maryam would say, "We weren't dancing!" meaning Afghan style, which means holding hands up, arms bent at the elbow, and waving the hands in a flowing manner, quite beautiful. And then Sakina showed a video they took of themselves dancing. I exclaimed, "What!" feigning shock. And then Maryam rolled her eyes laughing. It was good to see Maryam having so much fun. Later on, Maryam ended up not trusting her for some reason, and the relationship faded away.

Samira was small and short at 5' 2" and had the appearance of a waif moving silently through the world. She looked frail, and circles around her eyes were a bit grey. She was well along in her pregnancy, but you couldn't tell it even though she was small. She never told her dad she was pregnant, even after her baby was born because she was fearful of what he might say or do. How she kept the baby a secret I'll never know. She had the baby with a guy who didn't want anything to do with her. She was still in love with him and couldn't let go of him (think about Maryam's relationship with the rape guy). These kinds of relationships with a father and a boyfriend are well within the realm of Canadian culture, but they also deeply fit with the pattern of Afghan culture. Leila and Maryam had an on-again-off-again relationship. Very intensely close for a while, and then nothing at all. Leila had had her baby and, most of the time, put him in the care of an older woman but would visit him several times a month. She got a job and was making enough money to support herself but not enough to support her baby. They eventually lost touch with each other.

Esmatullah and Maryam met at the mall, exchanged their bad stories, and were drawn together by them. Esmatullah drove her back to our house, but slept in her car out in front of our house, turning heat on and off through the night to keep warm. In the morning, they came in to go to the toilet. Esmatullah was coming down the stairs when we first saw her, and asked, "Who are you?" She started to talk and then started to cry. She told us that her husband married her when she was fourteen, and then she came to Canada. She was about twenty-four at this point. She said he kept her in a room with just a TV and mistreated her. Maryam told us her story was worse than hers. She had two kids, moved out because things got so bad, and lived in a shelter for the first few nights. Then, she lived with a Pakistani family that was so horrid she went to live out of her car. I had heard about people living out of their car, but this was the first time I met somebody about it.

On hearing this story, Jennifer and I, again with our soft hearts, went up and hugged her and invited her to stay with us. She got her U-Haul, and within an hour she and Maryam emptied all of her belongings, including some bedroom furniture, out into our garage. We immediately returned the U-Haul to the dealer to avoid the next day's rent. At least she was smart about saving a buck. She was working nights at McDonalds down the street from us and had some kind of an affair with an Arabic-Egyptian guy she met there, and then there were other guys in just weeks. She really seemed to be wildly promiscuous. Previously, she had a series of low-level jobs. She was smart enough but had a poor self-image. She could have gotten more education but was not motivated to do that.

Her two daughters were seven and three, and they would come to be with their mother on the weekends. She loved them and wanted to have them with her, but she wasn't the greatest mother. Even the basics, like feeding them was marginal. Hours would go past what we thought would be a feeding time, they would come down hungry, and she had not prepared any food for them. She did not have the best hygiene—her body and her room really smelled. Yuk! Nor was she tidy. She really took to us as parent figures because she didn't have parents in Canada. However, she kept in close contact with her mother back in Afghanistan, but she had been in Canada since she was fourteen.

She wanted us to be the judge of her husband and determine that he was guilty of the wrongs he had done to her, just as she had described to us. She got us together at a restaurant, and after the meal, she explained her side. Then we asked him about what she had told us. He said he felt like he was being persecuted and then gave us his side. Quickly, it all escalated into arguing, and I said we needed to calm down or we would get nowhere. That evening, as time went by, it turned out that what Esmatullah said had less truth than she purported. There was some basis for her version of the events, but her husband came out a better person with a more balanced view. He had not treated her as poorly as she had said, and he was a good provider and father. The older daughter would talk about good things her dad did, him spending positive time with her and her little sister. After some months, to my surprise, Esmatullah moved back in with her family. However, when Maryam visited, staying overnight on weekends, she would come back saying she could not go back again because they argued so much. She often invited us to dinner with Afghan friends, and things were peaceable then, thank heavens. It was fun to be part of the Afghan social setting, have good Afghan food—the good parts of Afghan culture that we had not seen very much of.

One poignant thing Esmatullah told us was, "Don't trust any Afghan, *not even me*! Your best friend can stab you in the back."

Early on in their relationship, Maryam and Esmatullah figured out they were like 4th cousins and grew up about a 15-minute walk away from each other—one more long strand in the spaghetti bowl. After the big fight, Esmatullah turned on Maryam viciously, spewing some horrid lies about her to her mother back in Kunduz. Esmatullah's mother would pass it on to Shabana, and Shabana would bounce it back to Maryam, and then Maryam, of course, got angry with Esmatullah—a vicious circle indeed. What better example of the spaghetti bowl with nasty noodles. Three degrees of separation, half-way around the world. Periodically over ensuing years, Esmatullah would call Maryam and say some nasty things which hurt Maryam deeply. I'm thinking, just give it up girl, don't you have anything better to do than sow hate and discontent? I really feel this girl has some deeply seated problems, and I wish they were fixed. Maryam would say how much that aggravated her, and I would reply, this girl has a lot of problems, and you don't need her in your life. Maryam and Esmatullah had a really big fight; it was just a nightmare. That was the last time she saw Esmatullah.

Maryam met Baseerah at work. Baseerah lived with five of her adult siblings and her parents. She would invite Maryam to their family dinners, which Baseerah's mother cooked. Her mother loved having Maryam there, but the father was more aloof. It was good for Maryam, eating home cooked Afghan food with a big Afghan family, talking Farsi, sharing the culture—these were the good things about Afghan culture. Baseerah had two sisters in their early twenties. The first time I saw them out shopping, they were dressed in classy and provocative clothes. When Maryam was at their house, the three would say, "Hey, Maryam let's go to the movies", then they would go to a discotheque-bar. Maryam was underage, and they would sweet-talk the bouncer into letting her in. Inside, there was loud music, it was crowded, and boys and girls were dancing body-to-body. Maryam was not up to that at all. Baseerah and her sisters had tricked Maryam into going. She told Maryam to go out in the car if she didn't want to stay in the club. But it was cold and snowing. Not a good deal.

Another time, they tricked her into going to a hookah bar. This is where they smoke Turkish tobacco, enough to gag the initiated through a water pipe. Again, this was something Maryam detested. She would freak out if there was one person smoking, even in the next room. If she went outside, she would be standing in the parking lot all by herself, where she didn't feel safe. She called her boyfriend, and he was furious that they had tricked her. He was not fond of hookah bars because he thought that it was immoral. He jetted out and took Maryam away. So, with Baseerah, there were good times, and there were bad times.

Siddiqa and Maryam met at a Norouz party, the Muslim New Year, and instantly hit it off. An Afghan student at one of the universities in Toronto had started an Afghan Student Club and put together this Norouz party. I took Maryam to the party, and it was the first time I was in a room with a lot of Afghans, and I was a bit spooked—all of these twenty-something brown faces. I have been immersed with people of many different cultures and races, but this occasion spooked me. Siddiqa grew up in Moscow, Russia. As nearly as I could decipher, during the 1980's when the Soviet Union was fighting in Afghanistan, they had some factions of Afghans who supported them. After the Soviets left, they opened the door to some of these allied factions, and Siddiqa's father was in one of them. Siddiqa and two older sisters came to Canada only about a year previously and were living together. Siddiqa spoke Farsi and Russian but was just in the beginning stage of learning English. Maryam was much further ahead on that score, and they were about the same age. They spent a lot of time together, and she even spent a few nights at our house. But things went bad, very bad. Siddiqa turned on Maryam when she came to the courtroom with the rape guy. That was the worst thing any of her girlfriends did.

Hanifa and Maryam met at work and were friendly enough. She was in her early 30's. Maryam went and had dinner at her house a couple of times, and even invited Maryam to rent a room from her. She was more mature and seemed more stable than the younger ones. More mature but no less wicked. She was in the courtroom also, but it wasn't as hurtful because Maryam didn't have as close a relationship as she had with Siddiqa.

Boyfriends

The most horrific experience Maryam had with a boyfriend was with the rape guy, and thank heavens Maryam was able to move on past that relationship. The depth of the trauma was especially painful. Thank heavens, after that, there were two relationships which had their endings, but they were only slightly traumatic compared to the first.

Mohammad came into her life, and that relationship lasted nearly three years. He was respectful and kind to Maryam, just the opposite of the rape guy. They really cared for each other, and Jennifer and I thought this relationship had a lot going for it. He was an Afghan-Canadian, but there was one hitch, his mother. She was very deep in her Muslim faith and very conservative in cultural ways. She spoke no English, lived wholly within the Afghan community, and everyone she knew was from the social network emanating from the nearby mosque and back home in Afghanistan. She knew Maryam had been married before and therefore believed Maryam was "tainted" which led to her to forbid her son to marry Maryam. Over a period of nearly three years, Maryam met her once in contrast to our time with Mohammad, who ate dinner with us once or twice a week. The one time Maryam did meet the mother, they went shopping, and the mother would stay at least fifty feet away from her and barely say hello. After the relationship went past a year, Jennifer and I asked them, "How is this going to work? Mohammad, if you marry Maryam, that means you are essentially going to divorce your family. Your mother will have nothing to do with you." No answer. The attraction was just too great, they couldn't let go of each other.

Mohammad's dad had an Afghan kabob restaurant where he worked. He lived with his parents and brothers and sisters, further showing how tight he was with his family. Living with your parent's family as a young adult was more common than not for an Afghan family. He helped a lot of Afghans with immigration, medical, translation, and other matters, getting adjusted to Canada, a very helpful guy all of the way around. Going toward the third year that Maryam and Mohammad had been together, his mother had a plan to take him to Afghanistan for a three-month trip in order to find a bride. In Western culture, this would not be too likely, but this is Afghan culture. If he had learned more to the Western culture, he would not have gone. But this was the real test, and he ended up going with his mother to Afghanistan. For Maryam, this was the end. His mother clearly had control, and Maryam never talked to him again.

Moving onto boyfriend number three, Faizal. One summer day, out of thin air, Maryam came downstairs and said she was planning to get *married*. Jennifer and I exclaimed in unison, "*WHAT?!*" Maryam told us an Afghan-Canadian guy, Faizal, who had traveled in Afghanistan and met Sayeed. She told us Sayeed thought he was worthy of marriage to her and she would be a good fit with Faizal. After that, Faizal called Maryam, and they made plans to get married. We figured if Sayeed had met the guy and made a judgement that Faizal was a decent guy then, we guess, he's good enough for us. But it still didn't make sense to us. We were in shock that all of a sudden, she's going to get married.

Jennifer and I said to each other, "Wow!! that's a pretty big leap." But then we thought, under certain conditions that could work. If he came down on weekends, they got to know each other over several months and then made some kind of a decision. Gradual familiarization would be a good idea. Their plan was drastically different. He lived in Montreal, and he was going to drive down to Toronto the next week and take Maryam back up to Montreal. "*What the heck?!*" we exclaimed again. At that point, Jennifer and I were more than a little anxious.

Worst case scenario, he was a bad guy who somehow fooled Sayeed. We thought that all of the horrible stuff the rape guy did to Maryam could happen all over again. So, I wrote up a list of 13 questions for him to answer. Maryam sent the list to him. He asked, "What am I doing here, applying for a job with the Canadian Government?" He sent a copy of his driver's license, his work badge, and other stuff to the point I felt halfway comfortable.

Before he came down to Toronto, Faizal told us more of his story. In Afghanistan, his father was in local police and then the national military. He rose in ranks in the military to the level of general. He moved around with his family to Pakistan, India, Iran, and other countries. His father got on the wrong side during the Soviet occupation of Afghanistan and had to get out of Afghanistan and decided to immigrate to India. Faizal had several siblings, some older, some younger. They lived in countries all over the world, including Germany and Canada. He grew up mostly in Deli, India, in an Afghan community where they all spoke Farsi. He had a noticeable Farsi accent on his fluent English. When he finished high school, he moved to Montreal, stayed with an aunt and got a college degree in IT, and started working there. He said he had no previous wife or children. It seemed like a true story, but with the benefit of experience, we felt this was a story that was not true. Jennifer and I were very anxious about this guy suddenly appearing in Maryam's life, and they're going to get married.

The plan of Maryam and Faizal did prevail—he *did* come down to pick her up. He was thirty-three and seemed mature, with his feet on the ground. After talking for an hour, they packed up Maryam's bags. Standing away from the wall, in the big picture, there were way too many red flags. We just didn't trust what was going on. There had to be more to the story than what either of them were saying. Right before they left Maryam took us aside so Faizal couldn't hear and told us that she was going up for a one-month trial period to see how he was and that she wasn't going to tell him about her plan because that could alter his behavior. After she was up there awhile, she reported that he, his mother, and sister treated her nicely. At the end of the month, she told him that he was on probation and that she was returning to Wilmington. She told him she had two concerns. First, he needed to get a place separate from his mother and sister for them to live in. Second, he shouldn't be out of town so much because his plan was to be out of town a lot in October and November.

Once back with us, Maryam started to tell us the truth about what happened when she was up in Montreal living with him. The biggest thing is that he had a wife and two kids (though he was divorced), which meant he lied to us and Maryam—not a good basis for starting out a relationship. Maryam, by her own admission, had said for years she didn't want to be a mother because she isn't patient enough. Furthermore, she said she was not mature enough to take care of herself, let alone a child. Also, it came out very quickly that he lived with his mother and two adult sisters who were mean to her.

Over the ensuing weeks, we kept telling her about all of the downsides of getting married. She was really wrestling with this decision, and some nights, she got no sleep at all. The weeks turned to months. Since his trip to come down to Toronto to pick her up, he had not returned once. Finally, she flew to Montreal and told him no. He wasn't very happy about it, but that was that, and Maryam returned to Toronto. I told her this took an enormous amount of emotional courage, and I was so proud of her to take this step forward into a better life. Months later, Maryam told us that in the first week up in Montreal, she and Faizal got engaged. *Wow!* That was a shocker or us!! The good news is Maryam got out of it.

Months later, after that, Maryam fessed up that Faizal was very demanding. His mother made her clean every room, even after they were spotless, day after day—there was no way Maryam could please her. She made Maryam cook, which alone was enough to be a deal killer. The worst was a lie she told us in the beginning—Faizal never was in Afghanistan and never met Sayeed. The truth was that *Maryam found him on Facebook*—that's two boyfriends she found on Facebook. Then, down to the bottom of the truth—a month before she came downstairs to tell us she was getting married, she had taken herself off of Zoloft, her anti-depressant medication. This set off all of this aberrant behavior, culminating in looking for a husband. I told her, "Don't take yourself off of any meds unless you have a doctor guiding you. Bad things can happen."

Chapter 6: Sarya and Ibrahim

Sarya

Sarya is Maryam's niece, and Maryam has a strong relationship with her, like a little sister. They had this strong relationship before Maryam came to America, and in the years since, it has been reinforced with nearly daily phone calls. In 2000, Maryam was eighteen years old, and Sarya turned nine years-old when she was kidnapped by three young men. A couple of days passed, and our fear mounted that she was getting beaten, raped, or killed. Then the kidnappers called and showed a video of her being beaten up and severely kicking her. The next part of the video showed she was bound by her hand and feet in a chair sitting up, she screamed for mercy. Later Sarya pleaded, "I am just a little girl, what could you possibly want from me?" They said they wanted $10,000. Three days later, Sarya pleaded to one of the kidnappers, who seemed to her not to be as hard-hearted as the other two, "Can't you understand, my family is poor, you're not going to get $10,000 from them. They just don't have it."

Ibrahim is a cousin of Maryam's and close to Sarya. A few days later, the one kidnapper, who seemed to have a conscience, released her to Ibrahim and turned witness on the other two to the police. It turned out that the kidnappers found Sarya at random, not a family member carrying out a vendetta. The police knew these three because they had been convicted of kidnapping three times before. It was good news the police took action, which isn't always the case. We hoped these guys would be kept in jail for a while. Every time we thought we had hit the bottom of the depraved hell of Afghanistan, we found the bottom was deeper.

Sarya was very beaten up and had to go to the hospital for an operation on her two broken vertebrae, damage to her jaw, and a broken foot. We could only imagine how they caused all this bodily damage, which rendered her in great pain. The medical bill was about $5,000. Her mother sold $3,000 worth of jewelry, a cousin sent $1,000, and we sent $1,000. The kidnapping took place in Kunduz, but the operation was to be done in Kabul.

Ibrahim was prepared to help in any way possible, so Ibrahim and her mother and father, Malakaah and Nabibulah, took Sarya to Kabul. At least one of them stayed in the hospital room with Sarya around the clock. They stayed at an aunt's house when not on duty at the hospital. After about a week, Ibrahim went back to Kunduz to be with his wife, Salima, and his two little kids. Sarya was released from the hospital, and they were all at the aunt's house for a short time. Then Malakaah, Nabibulah, and Sarya returned to Kunduz. By this time, everyone could exhale and feel the full force of their grief. The doctor said it is these kinds of things that make Afghans want to leave Afghanistan. We took that to mean that this was not the first serious physical beating of a young girl he had seen.

One of Ibrahim's aunts found a counselor, Karima, who recommended sessions once a week. The cost was $100 for four sessions, not bad compared to the hospital costs. She sounded very good, and Sarya was comfortable with her. Sarya continued school by doing her studies at home, and the tuition was $150 per month. These expenses, plus housing and food, added up to $650 a month, which we were paying. These costs were worrisome to Maryam and started weighing her down.

ONE DAY IN AFGHANISTAN

Not yet ten years old Sarya was kidnapped again! The family went into a panic—once more. She was beaten to the point of unconsciousness and dumped at her grandmother's house, which meant they knew Sarya's family. It seemed to smell the hand of a bad uncle, Ramatulah. Beaten up severely at age nine twice?! Little nine-year-old Sarya felt enormous terror and trauma. Another trip to the hospital and more money.

Maryam returned from work in a very dark mood. She didn't want to sit and eat with us, and she wasn't talking. As is often the case, we could definitely tell something was wrong, and not much later told us what was going on. Sarya was so terrified; these animals had beaten her physically and demeaned her emotionally. Sarya wouldn't let anyone touch her and blamed everything on herself. Maryam said they weren't even animals; they were less than animals who beat her and turned her into a very scared little girl. She had pushed herself into a physical and emotional corner to protect herself and didn't want anyone to enter her space.

Maryam was a half a world away geographically but tightly bound emotionally and was overcome with grief, feeling she couldn't do anything to help. We told Maryam, "You have overcome so much yourself. Sarya has known you to be strong in the face of trauma and seen you rise up over some pretty bad abuses yourself. Sarya will find her strength, but it will take some time. You can't help it if you feel you are injured and beaten down yourself. Inhale, hold your head up, exhale, and move forward. Talk with your counselor, she is your doctor in just these kinds of things. And now Sarya has a counselor."

A couple of weeks later, Maryam was at work and called Jennifer—Sarya tried to hurt herself. Maryam said everyone in her family was completely out of their minds, sobbing, and grieving. Ibrahim blamed himself because he hadn't picked her up on time the day she got kidnapped. Maryam said, "I must inhale, and I must go to work because I need the money to send back home to Ibrahim, Sarya, and their families." Maryam was sitting on a chair, bowing her head over her knees in a profoundly sad and sorrowful posture. Again, she was very worried about expenses in general, but especially at this moment, the medical bills for Sarya. And she said that every time we thought we had seen the worst, then the next time comes, and it's worse.

Karima said they didn't have Zoloft, which was the antidepressant that has worked so well for Maryam the last couple of years. What to do? Within a week or so, Karima found a medication that should work, and she would be able to adjust the dosage as needed. The aunt's house where they were staying was forty-five minutes away from Karima's house, but Karima knew of a place close to her house with a rent of $250 a month, which was the same as their current rent. Those were all good reasons for Ibrahim and family to make the move. As the months passed, Karima, Ibrahim's family, and Sarya grew close to each other and essentially became like family.

A couple of weeks later, Sarya was having frequent, bad nightmares. One night, Sarya had a particularly bad nightmare, so Ibrahim called Karima, who came right away. Clearly, Karima was going the extra mile to take care of Sarya. Karima told Ibrahim and Salima to talk with Sarya whenever she has a nightmare and console her to help Sarya get through the trauma at hand.

When Sarya turned eleven, her father, Nabibulah, started taking steps to marry her off to the highest bidder. It's like a puppy mill—breed and sell. Sarya was beside herself, not just because she didn't want to get married off to a scary guy but also because *she was just eleven years old*. She knew what happened to Maryam at age thirteen and couldn't imagine it happening to herself. Marrying daughters off to get some money just isn't something that happens in Western society.

Seven evil acts on Ibrahim, his family, and Sarya

Ibrahim, on hearing about the intention of Nabibulah to marry Sarya off, set about to protect her by moving to another house where Nabibulah couldn't find them. In the ensuing three years, Ibrahim primarily, but also Sarya, his wife Salima, and his son and daughter, Aziz and Bibi (ages just six and four in the first of the three years), endured a series of traumatic events, some beyond appalling. It turns out that the central figure behind everything was Sarya's bad uncle, Ramatulah, brother of Nabibulah. I summarize those events here.

- Some guys came up to Ibrahim on the street at night and beat him up.

- Ibrahim had trouble getting a job for over a year. Maryam bought him a bicycle so he could travel further to look for a job. The first day he went to use his new bike, some guys grabbed him, beat him up, and stole his bike. Two beatings in one week is not a good week, even in Afghanistan. Perhaps Sarya's aunt Shakila, sister of her mother Malakaah, had a hand in this—a pretty nasty woman all by herself.

- Neither Shakila nor her son, Shaziar, knew where Ibrahim and his family lived at first. But Shaziar started tailing Ibrahim and found the location of the house. Some guys wearing masks burst into the house, threw all the possessions around the house, turned it upside down, and destroyed furniture while Ibrahim, Salima, Aziz, Bibi, and Sarya watched in fright and terror. Certainly, by now, with three horrific events, it was clear somebody was out to get Ibrahim and his family. But who? And why?

- The house caught fire for reasons that, at first, were murky. This stuff was very personal. There were just too many things happening to Ibrahim, Salima, and Sarya in a short period of time to think it was a coincidence. Because the fire was costly, Ibrahim and family had to move back with Malakaah and Nabibulah. This, of course, was a terrible situation because Nabibulah then had access to Sarya and could go back to work, marrying her off. Sarya was scared to death again. And lastly, Nabibulah is not patient with little six-year-old Aziz and four-year-old Bibi.

- The bad guys beat up Sarya and Ibrahim on separate occasions out on the street.

- Now, it gets much worse. They knifed Ibrahim three times in the gut. Excruciating pain, more hospital, and more money, not to mention a close brush with death. Maryam sent over more "emergency funds."

- Ibrahim got a job in a restaurant, and a gas stove caught fire and burned his upper body. This and the other six events had to be related. But the owner said it was Ibrahim's fault because it never happened before. The police got involved because the origin of the fire was unknown, and they asked for the video tapes from the owner. The owner said he didn't have any tapes, so police stopped the investigation. Then Ibrahim found out that Ramatulah was behind the fire, and he used his all-to-willing son, Shaziar, to implement this horrific act. The details start coming to light. He was in the restaurant the night before the fire and adjusted the controls of the gas stove so that when Ibrahim turned it on, a huge flame would shoot up. Shaziar paid off the owner and the police so that he would get off scot-free. Ibrahim had burns on over half of his body. After some weeks, the hospital released Ibrahim, so he, Salima, Aziz, Bibi, and Sarya moved to a house near an aunt of his. She was a good aunt, a doctor, and she attended to his medical needs as he recuperated.

Connecting the dots, each one of these seven events and the two kidnappings of Sarya pointed back to uncle Ramatulah and Shaziar. It just seemed the conniving and perversity would have no end. How can one human do this to another? They could have just kidnapped Sarya and married her off and be done with it. No. This is more a matter of suspended torture. It seemed that Ramatulah wanted to string out the torture to maximize the pain. I have described only the main points of these seven events, but the whole story was even longer and more horrific. You can imagine Ibrahim, his family, and Sarya suffered from *collective, serious PTSD*.

Ibrahim's good aunt figured out the real story of the restaurant fire and told the police. But the police had gotten paid off. So she went to the police at a higher level. Then she went to Ramatullah and told him he should make amends, at least financially, for all of the horrific things she had perpetrated. We appreciated the steely nerve of Ibrahim's aunt, but nothing ever came of her efforts. Obviously, sometimes life is not fair.

In the midst of all of this evilness, Mother's Day arrived, and Maryam gave Jennifer her Mother's Day card, handwritten,

"Thanks for being my Mom. My best friend. You and your love taught me how to be a good daughter, a good person, and how to love people. You have provided me with everything. You give me love; you nourish my body and my spirit. You never ignore me. You always give me attention. You gave all the love that I never got from anyone. I am so happy that I have you and Dad in my life. I love you with all of my heart." In the midst of barbarity, we find love.

Ibrahim's kidney transplant

Ibrahim had been at the edge of death for many months and in great pain, very great pain. Because his face was burned somewhat, he didn't want anyone to look at him, not even his closest family, Salima, Aziz, Bibi, and Sarya. He was embarrassed about how the burn scars have disfigured not only his face but over half of his whole body.

A couple of months after the fire, one of Ibrahim's kidneys failed. It was beyond the skill level of the doctors in Afghanistan, so his aunt took him to New Delhi, India, for a kidney transplant. The doctors medicated him heavily, so he was very groggy. When he was lucid, he said how much he loved Salima, Aziz, Bibi, Sarya, and Maryam, the most important people in his life. And they, of course, missed him. Jennifer and I said to each other, but not to Maryam, it will be a miracle he lives. They didn't have health insurance in Afghanistan or India at that time, so you had to pay upfront. Maryam sent $2,000 for his medical expenses, which she borrowed from me, but she really does give all from her heart. This girl gives when others all through her life have robbed her of so much of her well-being. Other family members chipped in even when they had hardly enough money to live on.

A few days after entering the hospital in New Delhi, Ibrahim went into a coma. At first, as we understood from Maryam, his own body put him into a coma. I thought those sons-of-bitches shoved him off the edge. The next day, Maryam clarified the coma was medically induced. On hearing this, Jennifer and I were still thinking he was not going to make it. We wanted him to live, of course, but these injuries are so serious. And then we're thinking of the evil behind this. Five days later, the doctors brought him out of the coma. Still, it's a touch-and-go situation. Another five days later, he had a *successful kidney transplant.* What incredibly good news! Jennifer and I kept thinking about the worst case, but he was on the good side of the events. India is known to be a place where people sell off their body parts or, even worse—kill people for parts, mostly body organs. That raises a moral question: Is it right to accept an organ from someone who has sold their organ or even been killed for the organ?

It was just getting too expensive to stay in the hospital or a hotel in New Delhi, so once he was well enough, Ibrahim and his aunt flew from New Delhi back to Kabul. Maryam sent money for the airfare even though they didn't ask for it. Right away, Salima, Aziz, Bibi, and Sarya went from Kunduz to Kabul to be with Ibrahim. They all cried because this was the first time they could be together since he had his kidney transplant. Once back in Kabul, Ibrahim's good aunt took him back in.

Each step of the way, Jennifer and I continued to be concerned that Ibrahim had so much damage to his body from the burns and the kidney transplant that it would be a true miracle if he survived. We couldn't tell Maryam our thoughts. Maryam had to hold onto the thought that he would live a full life. We could only hope that Maryam wouldn't get self-destructive if he died. It, of course, would be enormous grief for Salima, Aziz, Bibi, and Sarya. In any case, even right at that moment, Ibrahim had endured so much trauma it is sickening. Maryam said Ibrahim cried a lot. Given all that had happened to him, it was only too understandable that he would be deeply depressed.

Ibrahim's good aunt really had gone the extra mile to take care of him. She gave up working in her medical practice for many weeks. She was simply the most extraordinarily good person, especially as compared to those who were so bad. Also, she was furious with Ibrahim's mother and especially his father, who had rejected him because Salima was from a lower-class family. They had even rejected their own grandson, Aziz, and granddaughter, Bibi, and done nothing to help Ibrahim even though he had suffered so much over the last couple of years. They didn't even care that he was the best sort of guy with morals beyond reproach. They couldn't have cared less.

Every day, Salima sent pictures and videos to Maryam of Aziz and Bibi, going from crawling to walking, just growing up—all very cute. Aziz's vocabulary quickly became like that of an educated adult! And pictures and videos of Sarya dancing with her friends, combing her hair as a fashionable, grown-up lady. This really lifted Maryam's spirits and ours too. I asked Maryam about Sarya being out of school. Maryam said her teachers are okay with it. They gave her homework, and they knew she'd get it done because they knew what a good student she was.

The medications to ward off rejection had to be used carefully under a doctor's supervision, and the doctor had to be a specialist in kidneys, a nephrologist. It was uncertain if the medications would work. Jennifer and I wondered about the cost of the medications. Jennifer and I kept on going back in our minds to some realities as we knew from experience friends who had had kidney transplants. In Canada, even with socialized medicine, the medications could be $15,000 to $20,000 a month; and that was ten years ago, the last we heard. Possibly, they would be less now, and the cost in India or Afghanistan could be lower. We just didn't know. Again, we didn't talk about this with Maryam because we want her to focus on Ibrahim surviving and living. Later, we found out the actual cost of the medications ended up being less than $100 a month. We were amazed.

In the midst of this barbaric society that abuses women and girls unmercifully, *Ibrahim was the prince*. He protected Sarya, even at *great peril to his own life… and did so repeatedly*. Since Ibrahim got burnt by the stove fire, their assaults stopped. Maybe they just got it out of their system; we just aren't sure. Sarya felt guilty about the abuse Ibrahim had taken. Sarya knew that the abuse of Ibrahim and his family ultimately linked back to her. Ibrahim, Salima, and Maryam had repeatedly told her that it was not her fault. It's the evil ones in the family who are the guilty, the origins of the evil.

Sarya turns thirteen

Life went on, time passed, and Sarya had her first period just about on her thirteenth birthday, a perfect time of puberty, making the girl more valuable on the market of selling daughters. Sure enough, Nabibulah felt compelled to marry her off again. He was both nefarious and opportunistic. Maryam knew that now Sarya was a "woman", she would be even more valuable as virgin.

Another threat showed up at the door, this time amazingly *not* at the behest of Nabibulah. A 30-something Afghan guy now living in oil-rich Qatar had gotten very rich himself. He has heard about Sarya, seen a picture of her, and decided that it was good not for him to decide he wanted to Sarya. *You remember she is now just thirteen!* He came to Ibrahim's house and offered to move Ibrahim and his family, along with Sarya, to Qatar and pay for all of their living expenses, put them in a nice house, pay for Sarya's education—everything, make their life comfortable. Here is Ibrahim, barely able to provide for his family and his body and spirit brutalized by the bad uncle Ramatulah, and he said, "What kind of man do you think I am? I can take care of my family, and I will not let you look in Sarya's direction or have thoughts of marrying her. *Get out of here!*" What a man of pure morality.

Sarya heard by word of mouth that there was a young girl kidnapped and killed in Kabul. Sarya completely freaked out. This was one more chunk of PTSD on *Sarya*'s pile of trauma. She felt Kabul was less safe than Kunduz and wanted to return to Kunduz. She was torn because she was in Kabul to be with Ibrahim and their family to avoid her father selling her off, but then the possibility of kidnapping tormented her. A few weeks later, Ibrahim, Salima, Aziz, and Sarya returned to Kunduz. Once there, Sarya returned to school. To do an end-run on Nabibulah, Ibrahim took his family and Sarya to a "safe house" where Nabibulah couldn't find them so as to protect Sarya from her own father. It was also where the bad cousin Shaziar couldn't find them, and hopefully, it would work this time.

Next, Ibrahim found a school for Sarya. This was a very good thing to allow Sarya to learn, grow, and thrive educationally and emotionally. However, it turned out that there was another cousin of hers at the school, and she was related to the bad uncle. This girl told Ramatulah where Sarya's school was. It was Shaziar, and one day, he stood in front of the school, Sarya came out, saw him, and nearly passed out. Terror is better than killing because you can make it last longer. Which is worse, Kabul or Kunduz? Terror seemed to be everywhere. Ibrahim and family secretly moved to *yet another safe house* with a different school… *again.* They were essentially fugitives on the run.

More treatment of Ibrahim's kidney

A couple of months after the kidney transplant operation, Ibrahim had swelling in the area of the operation and had to go to Kabul for treatment. At first, his aunt, who lives in Kunduz, didn't feel she could go because she had missed so much work previously, but ended up going with Ibrahim to Kabul. Things got worse, and Ibrahim had to go to India, where there were doctors with more expertise than the Afghan doctors. His sister, who lives in Kabul, went with him, and the aunt returned to Kunduz. In the middle of this dramatic circumstance of Ibrahim's great need, his parents were still dead set against giving any help to Ibrahim or Salima. Ibrahim's father, of all things, called *Sarya* up and told her all the bad things happening to Ibrahim were because of her. *Sarya is a little girl!* It's not because of her, it's because of his evilness. The spaghetti bowl has some very vicious noodles. Sarya was, of course, distraught and feeling guilty. She has had to deal with those ideas even without Ibrahim's father harassing her this way.

The treatment done in India on Ibrahim's kidney was successful, and a couple of weeks later, Ibrahim was back in

Kabul with his family. The doctors there said he was ready to return to Kunduz, but he should not travel the six hours on the long and rough road between Kabul and Kunduz; he should fly back. The ticket cost $300, and Maryam got tired of paying for everything and told Nabibulah that he should pay. It was Nabibulah who was behind all of these problems. Nabibulah relented and said he would pay the airfare. Ibrahim and family returned to Kunduz, and Maryam asked how the trip went. Ibrahim said, "Well, we had to go by road." Maryam hit the roof, fuming that Nabibulah was a liar. Traveling by road caused enough physical problems, and he had to go to the hospital, which would cost who knows how much.

Ibrahim's normal disposition was quiet and gentle, but this time, he was so mad. Through the four years since he protected Maryam, Ibrahim had been a prince in all ways. He had been selfless, long enduring through all of the unmerciful physical, not to mention emotional, pain. But this is the thing he can no longer endure—the straw that broke the camel's back. He finally cracks, exclaiming, "You are no father. You don't care about anything but yourself. It's just money for yourself." A couple of weeks later, Nabibulah bought a wheelchair for Ibrahim, apparently because he felt guilty that he hadn't paid the $300 for the airfare. All of a sudden, Nabibulah is in the hospital…in a coma, possibly because of this latest round of stress. We hadn't heard anything about Nargiz in a long time, and then *Nargiz*, of all people in the family, jumped into the fray from out of nowhere and blamed Maryam. When Nargiz was in doubt about any new family problem, he blamed Maryam. For Nargiz, it was always the right time for a family fight.

About this time, Jennifer noticed Maryam's weight had dropped, which no doubt was due to the chronic stress.

Counseling was helping her work through that, but there was a lot more to work to do. Maryam had been in our lives four years at that point, she stayed in close touch with her family, which is an unending stream of trauma that just piles up on her mountain of past trauma. On average, she would talk for about one hour a day. She was constantly struggling to keep her head above the water to breathe. She just barely got enough figurative oxygen to survive. Over the previous several years, she had focused her emotional energy on Sarya and Ibrahim because of the violence they had faced. Ibrahim was hanging on a narrow edge of life and death. The heavy notion that Ibrahim may die was wearing emotional for those closest— Salima, Sarya, Aziz, and Maryam, not to mention Ibrahim himself. If Ibrahim dies, it begs the question of what would happen to Jamila, Aziz, Bibi, and especially Sarya. Sarya would be the one who would suffer the most if she had to go back and live with her parents, Nabibulah and Malakaah—it would have subjected her to Nabibulah trying to arrange a marriage. These thoughts, conscious and unconscious, put more weight coming down on all the other trauma Sarya had endured. Also, when Sarya suffered, Maryam suffered equally.

Karima, the counselor, advised Ibrahim to stay at home with the family and not get a job. That is, he needed to be there to protect Sarya so that she had a greater sense of security. Also, he needed to recuperate. However, that meant there would be less income to pay just for a basic living.

Within a year, Ibrahim's kidney was acting up again, and he went to the hospital in Kunduz. The doctor said the operation would cost $1,100. It was the standard practice that the doctor would not do the operation until he received payment, a rule I had become familiar with quite well. Ibrahim's father said he would pay it, but only if he went to Germany without Salima,

Aziz, Bibi, and Sarya. That way Ibrahim could start a new family. Ibrahim told his dad, "You should rot in hell. I will stay with the family I have, the family I have chosen. I will love this family, so I will stick with it." We were not used to hearing this kind of strong language from Ibrahim. Again, Sarya was crying because she thought it was all her fault. Salima and Maryam told her, "No, no, no, it's not your fault." Maryam was very angry at Ibrahim's father because he was so insensitive and looked down on Salima and Ibrahim. I felt like I wanted to go over there and beat the crap out of him. I "loaned" the $1,100. By this time, the loans to Maryam were way over what she could pay even working full time, so these loans turned into gifts.

Don't forget where this all started: seven unmercifully violent acts culminating in the fire which damaged Ibrahim's kidney. By four years have passed, and Ibrahim's health has improved and basically returned to normal. Amazing! All of the worst-case scenarios Jennifer and I had thought of had not come true, thank heavens.

Karima had been married a long time before she met Ibrahim and family. She and her husband had lived in London for some years, where she received her degree in counseling. Then she returned to Kabul to take care of her mother, and this is where she started as Sarya's counselor. Her mother passed away, at which point she, Ibrahim, Salima, Aziz, and Sarya moved to Baghlan, a couple of hours south of Kunduz, where she owned two houses next to each other. She lived in one, and Ibrahim and family lived in the other. Karima had diabetes for some time, hadn't taken care of it as well as she might have, and then she needed an amputation and a prosthesis, a total of $5,000. She asked for a loan which she would repay when she sold the two houses in Baghlan. I gave her the loan.

After some months, her health started failing. Karima made a will for her money and possessions, which were mainly the two houses, to go to Sarya and Aziz. She passed away in early summer. Soon after the Taliban took over the region, travel on roads between the cities was even more dangerous than before. Ibrahim was going to return to Baghlan to sell the houses, but travel was just too dangerous. This left my $5,000 loan unpaid. I had compassion for Karima, but I had to be a steward of my money too. It seemed like Afghanistan's instability made it a sinkhole for money. That said, Karima was a very compassionate person. She gave so much help by counseling and being a family with Ibrahim, Salima, Sarya, and the two little ones, Aziz and Bibi.

Why these acts of evil?

Over a period of three long years, Sarya's father, Nabibulah, orchestrated this string of heinous and evil acts on Ibrahim with the help of his brother, Ramatulah, and Ramatulah's son, Shaziar. In some cases on Salima, Aziz, Bibi, and Sarya were subjected to the attacks. Ramatulah directed Shaziar, and sometimes other henchmen, guys Shaziar paid to do the dirty work. These evil acts were because Ibrahim started protecting Sarya from her father, Nabibulah, who was doing everything he could to sell off Sarya. Collectively, they perpetuated ancient traditions of selling off daughters and attacking anyone who got in the way. As these attacks were unfolding, Maryam and Ibrahim became more and more confident that this was the case.

Then, there is another layer of the plot. Maryam had been in Canada for some years and was not accessible for an honor killing or any nonlethal kind of abuse. So why not abuse Sarya because she was accessible and a good surrogate? And if anyone got in the way of abusing Sarya, such as Ibrahim protecting her, then just abuse and punish him. Ramatulah, Shaziar, and henchmen have gone really up and over the top in punishing Ibrahim, his family, and Sarya. Sarya feels guilty about these attacks because she knows they are because of her. And Maryam has been punished indirectly because she is emotionally tied very strongly to the trauma suffered by Sarya and Ibrahim. This is the Afghan spaghetti bowl and ancient barbaric traditions at its worst. What lurks in the mind of the evildoers?

Chapter 7: Post-Traumatic Stress Disorder

Definition of post-traumatic stress disorder (PTSD)

An expert in the field defines PTSD as when "A person suddenly and unexpectedly devastated by an atrocious event and is never the same again. The trauma may be over, but it keeps being replayed in continually recycling memories and in a reorganized nervous system." The emotional state of Maryam and others in this story easily fits within this definition.[5]

A person suffering this recycling is subject to a self-fulfilling prophecy. "If you conclude that you must be a terrible person (because why else would your parents have you treated that way?), you start expecting other people to treat you horribly. You probably deserve it, and anyway, there is nothing you can do about it. When disorganized people carry self-perceptions like these, they are set up to be traumatized by subsequent experiences."[6]

Retarded emotional development

Jennifer and I have searched for explanations of Maryam's psychological and emotional state, how trauma has manifested, how the mountain of trauma emanates from back home in Afghanistan, what is going on in the minds of Shabana, the bad aunt, and Nargiz, and what has shaped their behaviors. Then there is Sarya, the trauma swirling around her and directly hitting her, especially at such a young age, and Ibrahim's steadfast instinct to protect and be kind. I find myself increasingly saying and thinking, "I'm not an expert, but I think I'm getting a pretty clear picture of what PTSD is all about."

I am in my sixties, and I feel as if I have lived long enough to have learned a few things. I think, hopefully without pride that I have learned through my own journey of life more about what emotions are, what psychology is about, and how social interactions play out. When you're young, each experience is new. As you grow older, you have more and more dots on the canvas, so you can connect them to form a clearer picture. You go from a sample of one to a sample of many, maybe even a statistically valid sample. So, with Maryam's story, I have strained to form a coherent picture of her, her family, and Afghanistan as a whole. She has gone through more stuff by the age of seventeen than anyone should live through in their whole life. The same for Sarya. The one book that is most excellent in explaining PTSD in its manifold dimensions is the book by Bessel A. van der Kolk, I quote above. As I have read through it and come across another dimension, I think, this is Maryam, this is Sarya! Spot on.

After Maryam had been with us for a year, LFY staff asked several couples who had taken in LFY kids to discuss what LFY could do to make a better transition from LFY to the adoptive family. We all said that, unfortunately, there was little transition. It was as if families picked up their kids at LFY, and that was the end of the story. We all agreed that the LFY staff was overwhelmed, just barely able to hold their heads above water. LFY struck us as if it was a hundred-ring circus with ten ring masters and thirty trainers trying to maintain order. This was all despite the fact that it was extremely well-funded. We parents felt like a lot of stuff slips through the cracks even while the kids are at LFY, let alone when the kid moves onto a family. It's not that the staff wasn't trying. It's just that there is so much to do. There were so many kids with needs so immense.

The other thing that came out of this meeting had to do with emotional maturation. The lead staff person who was educated and experienced in these matters said that whenever a kid has a major emotional trauma, and it doesn't get healed, it's pretty likely their emotional growth stops at that age. Four sets of parents validated this principle, saying the youth they had taken in exhibited this stunted maturation. But we didn't realize that was what was going on. We each had a sample of one. Since then, we've heard and read from other sources which validate this concept.

It didn't take us long to observe that Maryam showed several states of emotional maturity. Sometimes, she acted her chronological age, about eighteen. Other times, she seemed as young as thirteen. Then other times well into twenties. Then most astoundingly, butunderstandably, she displayed wisdom reflecting her traumatic life experience, trauma that nobody should have to live through. She would show these different ages at different times, sometimes as rapidly as within minutes of each other. By her fourth year with us, it seemed to us she had gradually grown more mature. The thirteen-year-old girl didn't show up as often. She was developing a more serious side, mostly having to do with supporting Sarya. By her eighth year with us, her emotional age closely and consistently matched her chronological age of twenty-five. Thank heavens!

Much of this maturation is owed to the consistent and excellent eight years of counseling that helped resolve her PTSD. I asked her how she was feeling emotionally, and she said she was feeling largely healed. Jennifer and I agreed. Two years prior, I was thinking to myself that she could be in counseling the rest of life, the trauma was so deep. But she said, "Yes, not that I don't have things to work on, but I feel a lot better. I don't feel so overwhelmed." Amazing! She can get angry in a pretty nasty way, but these outbursts are less frequent and less intense. Think of her role models, Shabana, Amir, Nargiz, the bad aunt, and the general Afghan milieu. It's just astounding, for all of the severe abuse Maryam has endured, she is fundamentally not an angry person. In fact, she has a big heart.

When she has the slightest amount of money coming in, she wants to take Jennifer and me to dinner. Also, she sends a lot of money home whenever she can. A good example is when she found out that a cousin was not able to play his favorite game, football, because he didn't have a pair of football shoes. So she sent him $75 to buy a pair, just so his life could be a little happier. At one point, she got settled into a steady job making more money than she had before, and she said she wanted to give money to a food bank for the needy. Then, she started to give ten percent of her income to the church, a tithe.

It took Maryam a long time with us for her to recount all of the different pieces of the story relating to the attempted honor killing. There were so many different details, and then drilling down in depth on them. Even after being with us for years, she would repeat the most hurtful part of the story when Nargiz was choking her, and *Shabana yelled, "Kill her!, Kill her!"* For Maryam, those words were more painful than all of the physical pain from the kicking and choking. And then, the angel came to rescue her from all of the pain.

Even as Maryam has been here in Canada for years, Shabana still does hurtful things to Maryam, and simply is almost never kind to her. If Maryam could just turn her back on her mother, but she hasn't. It's an inexorable force that holds her in place. Deep within her is that irrepressible, human need to be loved, nurtured, and cared for by anyone around you, but most assuredly *your mother*. This is fundamental to human nature. An ounce of human kindness… please, just one ounce. But Shabana is not forthcoming with any love or kindness, even after eight years since Maryam left Afghanistan.

There is the example when Shabana said she was going to send $300 for Ibrahim's flight back to Kunduz, and she didn't do it. Maryam was so mad, and even Ibrahim was mad. Maryam has said recently Shabana is no good, she just wants the money in any way she can get it, most prominent of which is selling a daughter to the highest bidder. But then Maryam keeps on talking with her.

As the seventh and eighth years were passing, Maryam started letting go of Shabana. Looking at this whole change of attitude over the period of eight years, I think that the healing of her emotional wounds enabled her to become a more mature and independent adult. Based on that, it has enabled her to let go of Shabana.

Shabana has been an unwitting instrument of her sister, the bad aunt. It seems that the sister has some kind of control over Shabana. Why this is so, we just don't know. There is no doubt something going on in the history of that relationship. Whatever the reason, clearly, the sister has control over Shabana. Perhaps, it is a matter of a strong and domineering sister over a weaker one. The bad aunt is wicked, ruthless, vindictive, vicious, and so forth. What lies within this person?

Jennifer and I have often said that if Maryam didn't call home to Kunduz so much and catch all the ongoing drama and trauma there, then she'd be better off emotionally. But all of this contact *since* she has been in Canada keeps piling up on top of the trauma *before* she came to Canada. If she had stopped taking in all of this trauma back in Afghanistan, she wouldn't have to work so hard to become healthier emotionally. But it simply is not in the cards for Maryam to let go of her family back there. The culturally determined, strong pull of family ties is too hard to resist. If you are born into the spaghetti bowl, it is very hard to get out. The slopes are too slippery.

Laughing on the outside

Before the time we even met Maryam, we had heard from LFY staff two contradictory things about this young lady. On the one hand, she had terrible things happen to her, serious enough to cause PTSD or worse. Her brother Nargiz nearly killed her to regain the honor of the family. On the other hand, we heard that she was outgoing and happy—everyone knew who she was at LFY and she knew everyone there. These two characteristics didn't jive. These were polar opposites. In her first year with us, she seemed to have "normal" behavior. She was more outgoing than average, for sure, and was even-tempered. In our house, her bedroom was on the second floor. Hers was at the top of the stairs which we had to pass it on the way to our bedroom. But we never opened her door except when she invited us in, say, for example, when she had put up special decorations. We wanted to give her privacy.

After she had been with us for about a year, it was morning, and her door was partially open. She was in bed crying, but still asleep. This was the first indicator that trauma lay beneath—after a whole year we finally got it. Later that day, I asked her about that. She explained that she maintained a happy exterior to cover up all of the pain from her trauma. It was her way of coping, which had worked very effectively. So effectively that *even we had no idea she was covering up–for a whole year.* She had this technique perfected. Later, there were times she fell asleep in the back of the car and would have nightmares. Sometimes, she would wake up screaming, visualizing a man, and sometimes men, coming to attack her. Jennifer and I were so busy helping her with ESL, schooling, and homework that we hadn't caught on to the PTSD, which was the barn door.

She told us that a lot of times, she didn't sleep well at night. But when we were going on car trips over twenty or thirty minutes, she would fall asleep quickly. Maybe because we were right there, she felt safer, or perhaps it was the hum of the car on the road. One time, she said there was a man holding her wrists, controlling her, and terrifying her. This particular nightmare repeated a couple of times. Sometimes, she was crying hard in her sleep but would wake up and not remember what happened. Then she confided that she had lots of nightmares, even more than the ones we knew about.

Jennifer and I are not professional psychiatrists or psychologists, but we felt pretty confident she suffered from PTSD. And once we took her to several of these professionals over the next seven years, they all diagnosed PTSD.

Mountains of trauma and the ocean

I have told Maryam many times, trying to assuage her trauma. I was trying to put her trauma in perspective. Then I wrote her a letter:

You, my lovely daughter, have endured many, many very serious traumatic events. By all accounts, any one of these traumas would be enough for anyone to be self-destructive, suicidal. In fact, you have tried suicide three times, but thank heavens you weren't successful. This man your mother married you off to, he raped you several times; you said, "No, no," but he raped you anyhow. Your mother married you off to a horrific marriage, which resulted in an attempted honor killing, at which she shouted, "Kill her! Kill her!" You hid from Nargiz, hardly eating or drinking anything for two weeks. You got on a plane to Canada, not quite sure what to expect; landed; got put in detention; got taken to a place with lots of young people disoriented and overcome by culture shock; not having anyone to speak Farsi to; and then the lesbian traumatized you more—*that is a lot of trauma.* Since you have been in Canada, you have kept in close touch with your family back in Afghanistan, including all of their trauma, which you have endured because you are so emotionally close to them.

One layer on top of another, *that is a mountain of trauma.* You have proved yourself resilient, again and again. You are a survivor. You are strong. Many psychiatrists and counselors have said you are the most resilient, strongest client they have ever met. You get shoved down, and you come back and say, "Everything will be all right." No matter how hopeless or impossible the situation, you come back and say, "Everything will be all right."

Maryam's trauma level is as if she is the ocean out to sea up to her neck, and one small wave can push her below the surface, nearly drowning her. She is resilient. She pushes her head back up above the surface so she can breathe, and another wave comes in, and the cycle repeats. She is one strong swimmer with enormous stamina and resilience. An ordinary person without PTSD can have a wave come in, and it's like they are up to their ankles in the ocean, and the wave is exciting, far from a traumatic event. They are at the water's edge, whereas she is out to sea. And the syndrome continues, "I may seem happy on the outside, but I'm miserable on the inside." However, psychiatrists have been medicating her with Zoloft for PTSD and depression for several years now, and she tells us she does feel much better, for real.

In the first year, Maryam was with us, she worked in a retail store, and guys would sexually harass her at least once a day and sometimes almost hourly. These weren't just young guys; they were often old men. It was a dark underbelly of retail that Jennifer and I were never aware of until Maryam explained her experience from the view of a young, attractive girl. This was just one more layer of stress for Maryam and was a daily topic of conversation at the dinner table.

After Maryam was with us for three years in Toronto with many, many Afghans, we moved a few hours away to London, Ontario There were virtually no Afghans there, and very few Muslim women wearing hijabs (the scarf over the head). (See Appendix 3 about hijabs.) Once there, she first worked at a grocery store. Maryam had three episodes of sexual harassment in a year, quite a difference from Toronto. One time, she came home explaining two big guys tried to corner her in a back corner of the store. She was incensed. I countered, "Maryam, in Toronto, you were harassed all day long." "Yeah, Dad, that was back then. Today is today." Then I realized, she's still up to her neck in the ocean, and she was just barely treading water to keep her head above the surface. At year six in Canada, she had recovered from her PTSD enough so that she was able to touch the bottom of sea floor with her toes. She still had a long way to go. Even at this point, I thought her trauma was so deep that she would be in counseling for the rest of her life. By year eight, I would say she was up to mid-calf, where it was unlikely that a wave would take her out to sea, a process much faster than I would have imagined. She is close to walking up on the beach and away from the shore. She is strong, persistent, and resilient. She is a survivor.

Many, many counselors and psychiatrists who have treated Maryam consistently have said that she has the worst case of PTSD they have ever seen. *Every one of them has cried when they've heard her story, and they are professionals trained not to cry.*

Trauma from back home

For eight years, Maryam has called home for at least an hour a day. She'll be on for an hour straight or on the line for a few minutes, puts them on hold for a few minutes, and then is back on. Often, she will have the phone on when she does household chores like washing the dishes. In effect, she is in constant touch, one step short of being in the same room. On the one hand, it has been good for her to keep in touch with her family, maintaining the cultural glue that holds the Afghan families together. It's an inexorable force. Family members are constantly coming and going in and out of each other's houses for short visits or long meals, a constant ebb and flow. In many ways, she just hasn't left. All that is good enough, but the downside is that she is hearing about all of the bad stuff, and it can be a little bad, or it can be horrific. (See Appendix 1, in which I explain the level of violence in the larger Afghan context. It's not just Maryam and her family.)

Maryam has been traumatized by just hearing about the horrific events happening to those she loves most dearly back home in Afghanistan. In other words, the events on the Afghan side traumatize Maryam as if she was there. There seems to be no end to the trauma emanating from Afghanistan. Consequently, Maryam never has had a chance to resolve her own PTSD which had accumulated since she was born. The problem is that current events back home have kept mounting up on top of the old. Afghanistan trauma is like the undertow of an ocean, it keeps pulling her back to deeper waters with high waves. Even if nothing happened back home, it would take a long time for Maryam to resolve the mountain of PTSD because of things that have happened directly to her. That said, she has had counseling for about six years by several different counselors, and they each have made their contributions to improving Maryam's emotional health. The counselor she had this last year has been most excellent. She listens and then gives pragmatic steps to resolve the issue of the day and move forward.

One morning, Maryam got the horrific news about the cousin to whom she gave soccer shoes. She was at work and got so upset she had to go home. Jennifer once more said,

Maryam do not take your phone to work with you. See what happened. You were at work for less than an hour, you answered the phone, heard the next horror story, fell apart, and had to leave work. If you didn't have the phone with you could have worked a full day. Your counselor has given you lots of good advice. 'Turn the phone off and the lights out at bedtime. Use white noise. Take 15-minute walks. Do all the things to calm yourself down. Breathe deeply. This will help keep anxiety and terror from piling up in front of you.'"

At one point, Jennifer, Maryam, and I started unraveling all the horror that Maryam had endured. Jennifer said, "All this trauma you comes from evil and Satan. Man's punishment can hurt, but God's punishment for sin, you won't want. Those who have caused this trauma will find out."

Not a week went by, and Maryam got a call at work that Ibrahim had had a traffic accident and was in the hospital with some severe injuries. After expressing my concern and sympathy, I repeated the rule: "If you are going to work, put your phone away; don't call home; don't accept any phone calls before or during work. Otherwise, it will disrupt work even to the point that you have to go home to recover." She said, "Yes, Dad-jan, I cannot afford to lose any hours. I need to earn money to send home." She is conflicted. She wants to keep up with the up-to-the-minute news from back home but wants to send them money for their unending needs.

Maryam attempted suicide three times

Suicide is, of course, the ultimate means of ending homelessness and PTSD. Maryam attempted suicide three Times in her first three years with us.

Suicide attempt #1: She drank a bunch of Pepto Bismol, and when we found out not long after, we took her immediately to the hospital, and they gave her an activated charcoal drink, which she did *not* like. It gaged her. She said she would never try to kill herself again because she didn't want to drink that charcoal stuff, which kind of made us think that this was a cry for help. Cry for help or not, a suicide attempt is flat scary. We wanted to get her behavior to be in good health. We had a big talk; told her how much we loved her; how devastated we would be if she had followed through, not to mention everyone back home. This just wasn't be the way to solve her problems. We figured she was just so depressed and hopeless, that she reached for the pills.

Suicide attempt #2: She attempted hanging with a scarf in her bedroom but realized it wouldn't work. We took her to the emergency room right away. They didn't have a psychiatrist at the ER facility, so they did a session on Skype. I was dubious about doing a psychiatric evaluation on Skype, whether it would work very well, but it did—it was as if the doctor was in the room. She had a very professional yet compassionate character and asked about Maryam's immediate situation and then the longer background. Her diagnosis was that Maryam had depression and PTSD, and was prescribed Zoloft.

Within days, it started showing good effect. Maryam told us she felt happy, she didn't feel hopeless. One change was she started keeping her room clean and orderly every day. She said she would never want to think about committing suicide again. (Sadly, we had heard this not too long before.) She told us how terribly down she had felt like nothing would go right. We couldn't figure out if there was any particular trigger or whether it was an accumulation of trauma that got to a tipping point. The latter would be very plausible.

Suicide attempt #3: The method Maryam used on this third attempt was to swallow a bottle full of Zoloft. The story leading up to this point goes like this. Three months earlier, unbeknownst to us, Maryam had taken herself off of Zoloft. This resulted in disastrous effects. This was when the whole relationship with Faizal started. After a month with him, she told him she was feeling "confused" and that this marriage wasn't for her. A few days later, she was up in her room. She took videos of herself swallowing the bottle of Zoloft, and sent them to the boyfriend she had just broken up with, Mohammad. He quickly called us and told us she was in her upstairs room trying to commit suicide. Jennifer ran upstairs; grabbed Maryam; and we drove lickety-split to the hospital emergency room.

After nearly twelve hours in ER, the doctor's decision was to put her in the "Behavioral Health Unit B," which is the place where they have people with chronic mental health problems. She resisted violently, and it took two big cops to manhandle her across a hundred yards from ER to Unit B. We came to visit her that evening, and she exclaimed that, "*These people are really crazy, I don't belong here!*" and that she wanted to get out of there "*NOW!*" Jennifer and I had no idea what raising a teenage Afghan girl was going to be like, but here it was! Maryam had permission to call us as much as she wanted, which didn't sound logical to us, but the rules allowed for that. She repeated again, "*Get me out of here NOW.*" We went up to visit her the next day in a visitor's room, where we could observe patients with outwardly abnormal behavior. We found out that this is what the chronically mentally ill look like. She was crying inconsolably and pleaded to go home. We told her we didn't have control of that; only the doctor could decide based on an evaluation. The next day, we went up and met with Maryam and her doctor. We explained our relationship and other key parts of her background. The doctor had definitely scoped out everything about Maryam's behavior. She saw right through her attempts at manipulation to get herself out of there, *NOW!* We thought the doctor was incredibly perceptive, insightful, and experienced.

The conclusion was to wait until the next morning when the doctor had a chance to review her case. Jennifer and I talked with the doctor alone, and she asked our opinion of whether to stay in the unit or not. I explained that I could see that the Behavioral Health Unit B is there for a reason, but I felt it could be more of a detriment to Maryam than it would heal, that is, it could aggravate her behavioral problem. Behavioral Unit B had a One-Flew-over-the-Cuckoo's-Nest feel. I told the doctor that if Maryam were in our house with us, there would be more of a calming effect. It would be an environment she was more comfortable with. The doctor agreed with us and decided to release her. We picked her up a few hours later. She was enormously glad to get out—a big group hug which we hadn't had for a while. For Maryam, the seventy-two hours in Unit B was forever. On the way home, she said, "I will *never, never* try to kill myself again! *I never want to go back to that place ever again.* Those people *ARE* crazy back there." She has continued to have mounting stress in the following years, but she has not attempted suicide. Five years later, she got much better, to a "normal" behavior and emotional state.

Maryam told her sister Jamila what had happened, and she exclaimed, "Don't you *ever, ever* try that again! It doesn't solve your problems. You're my little sister; you can't go do something that stupid! This would make our whole family *very, very sad.*" Very uncharacteristically, Sayeed exploded on Maryam, yelling at her. *"I did all these things to save you, and you want to go and commit suicide?!"* Then Jamila broke down crying at the thought of Maryam killing herself. Sayeed continued, "Listen, you live like a princess. Your Canadian parents provide you your own room; feed you; give you love; you can work; you have no reason to try to kill yourself." I thought to myself, Maryam did have it good in those ways, but she had all of the unresolved trauma, and we had her going to counseling to heal those wounds.

Maryam initially blamed her boyfriend Mohammad for the third suicide attempt but told us much later that she had taken herself off Zoloft, which led to her relationship with Faizal. And she told us that *she found him on Facebook*. We thought the true story was that she was wrestling with what to do with her years-long relationship with Mohammad; went off the rails; stopped taking Zoloft; found the first available guy; and took off with him. She was trying to get Mohammad out of her head and out of her life and thought she could fill the void with someone else. A perfectly dramatic rebound effect. When she ran off, she lost her health insurance. This meant that when she made her third suicide attempt, she went to emergency for twenty four hours, followed by three days in Unit B. The bill was nearly $3,000 for those four days, which we had to pay for out of pocket. It's small compared to saving her life, but it still hurts in the pocketbook.

Life is cheap

It seems that self-harm and suicide in Afghanistan are culturally acceptable or at least more acceptable than in other societies because of all of the trauma many Afghans suffer. There is so much abuse within the family that people get depressed and harm themselves or maybe even go to the extent of killing themselves. As this book and many other sources point out, females get more abuse than males. And by the same token, they are more likely to get depressed. There are killings in domestic arguments, as one might expect. However, there are also wanton, random killings, seemingly by a certain element of Afghans who don't have anything better to do with themselves. There is just no apparent reason in these cases. I conclude, *life is cheap in Afghanistan.* In Canada and more so in the U.S., I've heard of killing by gangs, or domestic violence or drugs, and that is bad enough. But, in these cases, at least there is a reason. Here are stories to this point.

I picked up Maryam at work. Her mood was very down. When something bad has happened, often she will say she doesn't want to talk about it, and then, moments later, she's telling the whole story. This is a normal routine. She launches in.

A cousin of hers was murdered. Even though there is this undertow that life is cheap and that killing is easy, it's shocking when it happens, especially to someone close to you. She says it was a cousin on her dad's side. Generally, Amir's side is the good side, and Shabana's is the bad side. Maryam grew up with this cousin, and they were just about the same age. He visited often and never did anything bad.

He was Amir's favorite nephew, and Amir was upset. The cousin was in Kabul with another family member about his age. Some guys grabbed them and took them to some out-of-the-way place and *tortured them.* This is a special twist in addition to just killing. They cut off their fingers and toes and then killed them. They wrapped the two bodies in plastic sheets, transported them six hours all the way back to Kunduz, and put them in front of the central mosque. The culprits identified the bodies using information on their phones. This mosque is the most well-known place in Kunduz and is very well-known all around Afghanistan. The father and many family members knew exactly what happened and who the culprits were. Even Maryam, all of the way here in Canada, knew. Even if the perpetrators were family members, the question is why? And even if it is a family vendetta, it is just so brutal. The father and those in the inner family decided to keep the information from the mother, at least for the meantime.

One of Maryam's cousins, with whom she had been close, had been married about a year. The cousin found out her husband had been cheating on her, which led to a big argument. He threw a computer at her head hard enough that he killed her. As usual, *he* punishes *her* for his transgression. She was twenty-two, and he was twenty-seven-years-old. When Maryam heard this, she cried unconsolably. Jennifer and I gave her a big, long hug. Maryam caught her breath and moved onto the next topic. Is this resilience or just stuffing down the emotion or some mix? If Maryam went a week without some horrific news from back home, it's a good week. In any case, it is the only way she has been able to survive. .

When Maryam was about twelve, back in Afghanistan, she and some others of her family heard commotion down the street, and they went down to see what was going on. The story was that a girl had gotten kidnapped, and the perpetrators had *dismembered her*, wrapped her in a plastic bag, and left her body on the doorstep of her family. Whether a random killing or tribal vendetta, it's still an atrocity. It's one more example of how depraved the culture is. It just makes my blood run cold.

In Maryam's first month with us, Amir called and passed on news from back in Kunduz. Some guys kidnapped another *twelve-year-old girl, dismembered her*, put the parts in a plastic bag, and put it on her parent's doorstep. It's the same modus operandi as the last one, but about five years apart. I just burst out, crying my guts out. I thought, "What the hell kind of country is this." Amir had just told Maryam this story, and even he said, "I don't understand what's happening [here in

Afghanistan]." And the stories keep piling up, further validating this horrific thought.

Just one month later, she got off the phone and was crying, very hard. We asked her what was going on. She was talking with her Afghan dad, who told her that a girl down the street, whom Maryam knew and was her age, had an argument with her husband. *She poured gasoline on herself; set herself on fire; and killed herself.* Jennifer and I were simply stunned, just shocked. I just doubled over crying. In our lives, we had never heard of such a thing. We were waiting in a doctor's office when Maryam unraveled this new story. In this situation I normally wouldn't cry, but this was way too much. Amir said it seemed like things were getting worse.

Maryam had a cousin who had trouble with her husband a few years ago. It was so bad *she poured gasoline on herself and set herself on fire.* She died a few days later. The husband didn't directly set her on fire. but, I think it was because he abused her so much that she felt her life was hopeless and decided to end it herself.

In her sixth year with us, Maryam told us about another cousin who was in her mid-thirties and had three kids, ages eight, ten, and twelve. Her phone rang, her husband picked it up, and there was no one on the other end. He suspected a lover of his wife. In a fit of jealousy, he *poured gasoline on her from the head down and set her on fire.* Her organs essentially exploded on fire, *and* their kids were watching all of this. The husband escaped to Pakistan. Police tracked him down and returned him to Kunduz local police who put him in jail. It was remarkable he got jailed, given that men can act with impunity. I'm not sure if he got tried and convicted. A Canadian friend of mine rolled his eyes, essentially saying, "What the heck is going on over there in Afghanistan?"

Maryam has told us about other cases of females setting themselves on fire. That just baffles my mind. It seems like self-immolation is acceptable within the culture. I said, "Maryam, I think this is the third time in six years you have told us about a husband setting his wife on fire. And this is not counting the ones six years before that." She says, "Yes, Dad, that's right." My God, my God, deliver us from this evil.

Let's count this up. One torturing and killing apparently by a gang, one homicide by throwing a computer at the head, two homicides by dismemberment, two homicides by setting wives on fire, and one suicide by self-immolation, all in the span of twelve years, events known by one girl! What else is going on out there? Is this a representative sample? This is not abuse perpetrated on Maryam. This is violence going on in the surrounding community; violence within families; murder by a husband on a wife; and self-destruction by a wife with a fatal loss of self-worth. This all happened within the knowledge of one person, Maryam. How much would there be if you extrapolate to the whole country? (See Appendix 1 for the broader social context.)

In any case, these have all impinged on Maryam's psyche. It is trauma piling up layer upon layer of Maryam's PTSD. I think the prevalence of this depravity normalizes the behavior, makes it seem OK, and makes it harder for her to heal emotionally.

Life is cheap.

Trauma and counseling

In Maryam's first year with us, she told us "her story," which was the attempted honor killing; the escape from Kunduz to Kabul and onto Canada; detention at the Toronto Airport; and life at LFY. She told us the main part, the pieces, the details—*all of it without emotion*—which we didn't understand at the time. How could she be telling us about this very traumatic stuff that happened to *her personally* and not just bawl her eyes out? Years later, I was reading a book that explains that "traumatized men, women, or children" can react to the trauma "with blank stares and absent minds, the outward manifestation of the biological freeze reaction. Depersonalization is one symptom of the massive dissociation created by trauma."[7] This fits Maryam to a T.

Further to this point, Maryam's lack of emotion is consistent with a relevant study, also in this book, on trauma and youth, which compared youth who were not abused and those who were. In recalling a stressful event, nonabused girls showed emotion while "abused girls shut down and became numb."[8] Also, I have talked with experts in the field of trauma in children and ACE (adverse childhood experience), who say this this book is one of the most highly regarded in the field.

Jennifer and I would sit there bawling, but she talked without emotion. Over the years, several different counselors told Maryam that it is okay to cry about anything that disturbed her. As time went by, she was more and more able to cry freely. Looking back on things, we thought Maryam probably hadn't cried at all in her first 16 years in Afghanistan with her family because things were so bad that *not crying was the only way of coping*. Back in Afghanistan, if she cried, it would probably make her feel weak, and she had so many bad things coming down on her that she felt she had to stand as tall as she could and not cry. Shabana and the other evildoers probably would have shouted at her about how weak she was if she cried.

After Maryam's third suicide attempt and the diagnosis of PTSD and depression, we set about to find a counselor. I couldn't believe it took us that long to figure out that we needed to get the counseling. The counselor turned out to be outstanding. She listened carefully and then gave some pragmatic steps to help solve the issue of the day. Not vague or ethereal, just pragmatic: state the specific problem and offer an appropriate solution. She resolved so much of Maryam's trauma and set her on a path to a healthier life. As the years went on, Maryam had several more counselors, each of whom had their own techniques. But they followed the same basic method of listening and then offering pragmatic steps to heal. Several told her it's okay to cry. Maryam did learn how to cry, and she did get better. Often, she would walk out of a counseling session crying, and she would say in so many words, "That was painful, but I feel better now." Each counselor helped Maryam immensely. Counseling gradually would peel back and resolve the layers of trauma. The most recent counselor used the same method as the first to her great benefit.

Maryam told us she grew up never hearing about counselors or even the idea of counseling. Yet, having arrived in Canada and given the opportunity to have a counselor, she took to it instantly. She recognized that she had been traumatized just about all of her life, and counseling was a way to fix it. She took to psychiatrists the same way, including medication. She felt very positive about the antidepressant and nightmare medications that they prescribed. She had some Afghan girlfriends who demeaned her for going to counselors and psychiatrists and taking psychoactive medications. These so-called girlfriends said, "You're not crazy! You don't need a counselor or a psychiatrist or any medication." Maryam told them, "I have been traumatized and have some serious PTSD, and I need to fix it. So just buzz off!!"

Chapter 8: Violence in Maryam's Family and the Bigger Picture

As Maryam narrated her story through the years, I kept wondering, "Is this just her? Is this just her family? Or does her story reflect the larger Afghan society, the larger Afghan context?" Many Afghans I met through Maryam have explained that it is not just her family. Many of Maryam's Afghan-Canadian girlfriends have treated each other horribly, transferring these behaviors intact from Afghanistan to Canada, clearly corroborating abuse in Maryam's life back in Afghanistan. Many of them have told me the consistently same story that forty some years of war has ravaged social fabric of Afghanistan. While these explanations corroborate each other, these are still individuals, and they are still anecdotal explanations. I have a lot of evidence about Maryam, her family, and her community. But I kept asking myself, "Is Maryam's family and the consistent anecdotal stories enough to say it represents the larger society?"

To answer this question, I have reviewed studies and articles which provide a bigger picture of the violence and abuse of women and girls across Afghanistan suffer. These sources provide an ample and consistent context of primeval, vicious violence against women and girls. They stem not just from recent decades of war but, more importantly, from ancient tribal traditions and practices deeply embedded in the culture.

One dimension of this part of the culture is carrying out vendettas of one family on another family, which often turns out to be violence against a girl or woman who is only tangentially connected with the family members involved. These many sources corroborate each other—Afghanistan is a barbaric culture that regularly suppresses women and girls, including the worst violence, namely rape and honor killing. One of the most appalling acts is when women and girls who find no way out of their horrid situation and commit suicide. This includes, in my mind, the worst method of all, which is to set themselves on fire.

The Taliban are violent by nature, and they are well known for their suppression of women and girls. They are barbaric, to say the least, as the media has let the world know how extreme their methods are. They took over control of Afghanistan in August 2021, enabling them to add a regressive overlay on top of a society that already exhibits too much abuse and violence against women and girls. The worst example is when the Taliban was in control in the late 1990's, and they committed public beheadings in a filled stadium.(See Appendix 1 for a detailed description found in these sources.)

Chapter 9: The Taliban Comes to Town and the Family Runs for Their Lives

A warning about this chapter

There are many *very gruesome*, *graphic* descriptions in this chapter, so don't read it if sensitive to this. It would make what has happened before in this book seem like a kindergarten party.

The Taliban took over and the family hid in cellars

Ismail is a cousin of Maryam's and is close to her. For about a year, Ismail and family lived in a small city near Kunduz. They had moved there because Kabul was becoming unsafe because of the Taliban. Ismail heard the Taliban was about to come, so he determined that Kunduz would be safer, and moved his family there on July 15, 2021—a lot of moving around. The family group making the move were his wife, Nasima, daughter Aisha (age fifteen), and son Ali (age twenty). It was a Saturday, August 12th, that the Taliban took over Kunduz. To escape, Ismail and family were going to fly from Kunduz to Kabul and then to Turkey. Maryam had told me that visas to Turkey cost \$2,300 for six; then she corrected that to \$2,300 per person, which meant sending all four was way too expensive. Next was the idea of sending Aisha alone to Istanbul and having her stay with a young uncle. But that didn't seem good because he couldn't protect her all of the time because he'd have to go to work at some point. And the final piece in the Turkey puzzle is that Turkey changed its visa policy and didn't let Afghans in by air or ground. On August 15, 2021, the Taliban took over Kabul and almost all of the rest of the country. The situation was dynamic, to say the least, and even the best experts were kept second-guessing, including President Biden's military advisors.

That same day, August 15th that the Taliban took Kabul over, the U.S. was not letting commercial flights in or out of the Kabul airport. At that time, the U.S. had about 5,000 troops, and it was doing its best to get those troops out, get Americans out, and any Afghan personnel who had helped the U.S. war effort, such as interpreters and their families. Within two weeks, they had evacuated about 120,000 individuals—a herculean airlift. The Taliban also closed land crossings to other countries. Ismail's plan changed so that they would fly from Kunduz directly to Delhi, India, for $1,800 for four. Ismail and Nasima had passports and had gone to India before, so this was the last remaining possibility right now. The uncle in Istanbul was working on his end to get tickets from Turkish Airlines for them to fly to India. The week prior, the airport in Kunduz was open. At first, Ismail thought about staying with an Afghan family they knew in Delhi, but then on reflection, Ismail decided it was a no go. Everything was all a panic to flee from the Taliban as soon as possible to the best country possible.

Random bombings, which the Taliban had carried out for twenty years leading up to 2021, were one thing, but then it started getting personal. The Taliban accosted and beat up Aisha as she was walking to school because she didn't have the right kind of hijab. Not much later, they stopped her again applying more restrictive rules about the hijab. The rules were at the whim of the Taliban marauders on the street and not necessarily an edict from the Taliban high command. Then things got more serious. The Taliban busted doors down and marched into their houses, and kidnapped Maryam's older brother, Nargiz, and an older uncle, for unknown reasons. One thing you could say for sure is that the Taliban was short on rational behavior.

In the meantime, Aisha and Ali, Ismail, and Nasima went into hiding in an unfinished cellar basement. Ismail and Ali were in the front part of the cellar, covering a false wall behind which were Nasima and Aisha, the last defense against the Taliban. In the evening, when the coast was clear, one or more of them would come upstairs to eat and get some fresh air. This was just simply a scared family in a scary, terrorized country.

Again, their thoughts turned to ways to find safe passage out of Afghanistan. I sent a text on August 16th to fifty of my family and friends in Canada, telling them of the harrowing news from Afghanistan. I got many responses, and several replied that they were praying. I was surprised that the two said they were praying because I didn't know they were believers. I guess when the threat is big enough, you show your beliefs. At this point, prayer is what is left. The Taliban is evil to the depths of darkness. I hoped all of those prayers and wishes would lift them out of the fear of darkness into the light.

On August 16th, the Taliban knocked the doors open, burst into their houses, and kidnapped Maryam's uncle, Hazrat.

Humanitarian visas to Canada

Jennifer and I were thinking intensely as the events in Afghanistan rapidly unfolded. We thought we had to get Aisha out of there and to Canada to stay with us. On August 18th, I emailed an attorney with a law firm who had helped get Maryam asylum, asking if there was a way to get Sarya a visa to the Canada. The answer was *yes!* We couldn't believe it, a ticket to safety for the most vulnerable in Maryam's family. This started a flurry of emails with a team of six attorneys in offices across the Canada working to get the special "humanitarian parole" visa (HP visa). Only a few qualify for this particular type of visa. As with Maryam, the firm worked *pro bono* (for free, for the good). They would ask for information such as a copy of a passport, then I would ask Maryam, then she would ask Ismail, and then passed the information in reverse; and so it would go with many documents for three intense weeks. A critical part of the application is an affidavit of financial sponsorship with proof of adequate finances to support the applicant. Jennifer and I signed as sponsors. The law firm submitted the application on Sarya's behalf on September 7 to the Canadian Immigration Service (CIS), which is under the Canadian Department of Foreign Affairs. The law firm even paid the $575 application fee. I can't say enough about the dedication of these attorneys. They were sending me emails at 8:00 in the evening and on weekends! We heard through the grapevine that they were preparing over two hundred applications *pro bono* for Afghans trying to run from the Taliban. *Huge compliments to this law firm.*

With Aisha's application submitted, Jennifer and I discussed bringing over Ali (now age twenty). We had enough bedroom space, and we mulled over financially supporting them once they got to our house. We concluded that we couldn't just leave him there. I explained the Ali's situation to the attorneys and asked if they would be able to submit an application for him. Again, the answer was *yes!* We went through the same process, and the attorneys submitted the applications on October 28th, 2021. The CIS routine deadline was ninety days for review and decision of approval or denial. A little later, that changed to 120 days. So we waited. Then, at the end of November, the timeline was "indefinite." Frustration, blocked goals, but all we could do was wait.

Taliban committed violent atrocities on 14 of Maryam's family members

Maryam told us some pretty nasty stories about the tribal brutality *before* the Taliban took over. It turned out to be just ghastly, and because of this, I have told the details to only a few people. Within a month after the Taliban took over Afghanistan, the Taliban had committed these atrocities on 14 of Maryam's family. Here they are.

- They kidnapped and tortured cousin Habiba and Hazrat, an uncle, by pulling their toenails out. The Taliban picked Habiba because he had worked for the US military for a short period of time.
- Four Taliban sodomized a five-year-old cousin, a daughter of an uncle on her dad's side.
- They beat a twelve-year-old niece to death, who was the daughter of her Hazrat and his wife Shima.
- They dismembered an eight-year-old niece who was the second daughter of Hazrat and Shima. They put the remains in a plastic bag and returned them to Hazrat and Shima's doorstep.

- They beat her Hazrat severely with what looked like a 2 x 4, branded him with a hot iron, and sodomized him because he was wearing blue jeans. See Figure 1.

- They severely beat Hussein, Nasima's father.

- They shot Hamid, a cousin, ten times and Ismail two times when they went to another town looking for food. They had to go to the hospital, and Ismail got discharged after a few days. We were not sure how Hamid, with ten shots, could survive, but miraculously, he was discharged from the hospital after two weeks.

- About fifteen Taliban raped her sister Nasima, Aisha, and Shima laughing hideously while they forced twelve kids, ages fifteen to two-years-old, to watch. The three women went to the hospital immediately, but they were turned back because the hospital already had too many who were beat up or worse yet.

- They busted the door down and beat Zalika, Nasima's mother, hard with a rifle butt.

- They grabbed Hamid off the street a second time, beat him up severely, and sodomized him.

- They kidnapped Hussein and, after a week, returned him, beaten really bad fingernails and toenails torn out.

The Taliban told Hussien he had worked for a foreign organization. He lied and said no. They looked all over for the documents that would prove it. When the Taliban were coming to Kunduz, Hussein had hidden the documents, knowing they would punish him for that. How the Taliban knew what particular jobs particular individuals had done even years before, I have never been able to fathom. Do they have some kind of database and computer spreadsheets? In the end, it didn't make any difference; they punished him anyhow. They kicked him so hard in the back that they injured one of his kidneys, which needed to be removed. Shazia went to the hospital in Kunduz, but the Kunduz hospital was overwhelmed with patients, and this kind of operation was beyond their skill level. So he went to Kabul for the operation which costs $3,000. He was sixty-two years old, so the whole ordeal was all the more stressful.

Aside from beating, raping, and killing, Maryam told us the Taliban burned all of the crops and farm produce that her one aunt owned—walnut trees, fruit trees, and produce plants. This is food that could feed people, and you don't regrow such trees and plants in one season. If they had done this throughout the country, it would leave an entire population without these essential foodstuffs. Also, news reports said they had destroyed infrastructure, such as roads, schools, and hospitals, built by the U.S., just because the U.S. built it, further destroying much-needed infrastructure that would enable positive economic functions. It's hard to find the rationale, but then the Taliban is not a rational force, nor are they a benevolent regime.

Soon after her rape Shima was so distraught she poured gasoline over her head and was holding a lighter to set herself on fire. Hazrat was in the same room and grabbed the lighter away. Maryam told Shima that suicide is not the way. "It will harm all of those who love you. Your husband, your kids, your parents, your brothers, and sisters." This kind of psychological impact is often overlooked by media because the focus is on the direct atrocities, and they are gone once the worst atrocities have happened. The direct atrocities simply overshadow the indirect impacts.

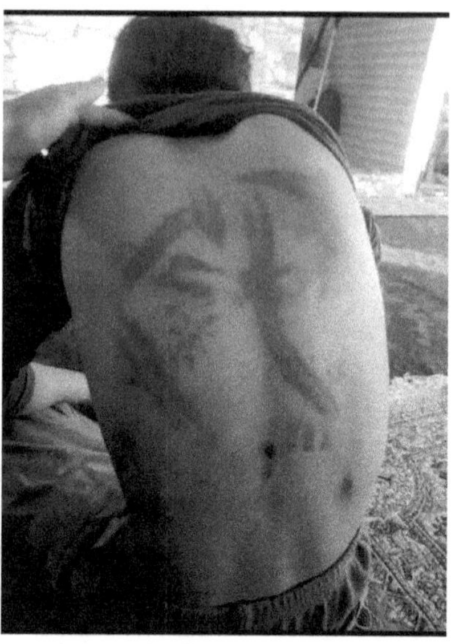

Figure 1. Hazrat's back after the Taliban beat him with a piece of wood like a 2 x 4 and branded with a hot iron.

(Photo courtesy of author.)

Maryam started having fainting spells

Since the start of the atrocities in mid-August Maryam started fainting spells. Any of us could be standing right beside her, and she would simply pass out and crumple to the floor for several minutes. In the initial episodes, at first, we weren't sure she was breathing. She was so still. Then she would start coughing and get super thirsty as she was coming out of unconsciousness and delirium. When she came to me, she would inhale about 8 oz. of water. This went on for about ten days. She went to her counselor, psychiatrist, and her regular doctor. She had a long weekend off and got better. She had a sleepless night, woke up nauseous, and vomited once.

Van der Kolk has a description of the psychological-physiological reaction. "We can speak of trauma when [the physiological] system fails: when you beg for your life, but the assailant ignores your pleas…when you see your buddy trapped under a piece of metal that you're not strong enough to life… immobilization is at the root of most traumas… Your heart slows down, your breathing becomes shallow, and zombielike, you lose touch with yourself and your surroundings. You dissociate, faint, and collapse."[9]

She was feeling so nauseous one day she called into work to say she couldn't make it. She had been working at a clothing store since early August, starting at $14/hour, a dollar higher than the grocery store where she last worked. They gave her full-time, which the grocery store never did after three years. *Plus* her second level supervisor at the department store was super understanding of Maryam's PTSD because her daughter had PTSD. It gives pause to think about how many out there have PTSD. Her supervisor is also empathetic, knowing all of the trauma brought on by the Taliban in Afghanistan. Many of her customers are aware of Taliban because it has saturated the news.

Six weeks later, by now, at the end of September, Maryam would continue to faint, fall onto the floor, hit her head, and end up with bruises and scratches. Jennifer noticed that there was something going on besides scratches from hitting the floor. There were marks a couple of inches long on her face and neck. Jennifer suspected Maryam was hurting herself with something dull, not anything sharp like a knife or a razor blade. Jennifer gently asked her about these marks. After three denials, Maryam admitted she was using a comb to hurt herself and said she didn't want to tell us because she feared it would hurt us. She apologized. We said, "No, no, this is not your fault." She said she felt so guilty that Nasima and everyone were suffering, but she didn't, so the only thing she knew was she had to suffer by her own hands. I think this is survivor's guilt. The Taliban atrocities have had secondary ramifications right into this girl in our house. What to do? We pray every day for her healing, it seems the only power we have.

By mid-October, Maryam had seen:

- Two GPs who basically recommended trying to resolve her anxiety and think positive thoughts.

- Her main GP several times for follow-ups and referrals.

- Her psychiatrist, several times who, adjusted her medications.

- A neurologist who evaluated her for epilepsy (negative), an EEG for brain wave abnormalities (negative), and a tilt table for I forget what (negative). He said these were just to rule out any neurological symptoms. He asked what would happen before she passed out. She said she would have bad images in her mind. He asked what kind. She said, "My niece was…" sort of reaching for the right word. I said, "dismembered." He leaned back, sort of internally gasping for air. The personality of this doctor was stable, steadfast, not one to rush to judgment, sober, and compassionate. However, the idea of dismemberment set him back some—not something I think he had heard of every day or may ever.

- Cardiologist who evaluated her echocardiogram (negative).

- Her counselor, who for over a year previously had been working with Maryam on her anxiety, depression, and PTSD and now has one more layer to work on.

I grew frustrated with the local doctors not diagnosing and finding a cure. I thought it was possible and was determined to go to a higher powered medical school and get some answers. Ultimately, I changed my mind. The last doctor, a cardiologist, said you can go there, but they will go through the same tests with the same conclusion. The diagnosis of fainting all came back to the stress of news about the Taliban committing atrocities on her family. Maryam had overcome trauma for all of her life with her incredible resilience, but my interpretation was that the Taliban pushed her over the edge. After what seemed to be too much time, the conclusion was to focus on getting rid of the images, primarily through counseling. The counselor whom Maryam had been working with was most excellent. She listened carefully and came up with pragmatic solutions, remedies. At least we had that going in the right direction.

By February 2022, she had not been working since September and, all along, was quite anxious to get back to work so she could support herself and help send money back to Afghanistan. All along, since well before the arrival of the Taliban, we had been paying for various expenses back in Afghanistan, and now, since the Taliban, we had been paying for her rent and expenses. So she just sort of willed herself to get better. By mid-February she had gone seven days without fainting, and her family doctor gave her a permission slip to return to work. But within two weeks, she had fainted twice, and the department store told her to go on sick leave until she got much better. They continued her health insurance, which was a big help. Eventually, after a few months, even that department store said they would need to take her off the roles. That store stuck with me much longer than I would have believed.

By September 2022, it had been a full year since the Taliban took over, and since Holly, for most of that time, had not been working, but she persevered in her usual resilient fashion. A couple more months passed with only a couple fainting spells. She got another job and has been with it for over a year with only a couple of fainting spells. Life is better in this realm.

Taliban atrocities on top of an ugly baseline

The hell that the Taliban has brought down is another layer on top of hell that has existed before their takeover. Here is another example. There were series of events going on with Asadullah, age sixteen, another nephew of Maryam's that were just horrific.

A high school teacher told Asadullah to stay after class, and it so happens the school was empty then. The teacher started touching his upper body, his face, and then his genitals. Four boys came in and tied a scarf around his mouth so he couldn't yell. The teacher and the four boys proceeded to gang rape Asadullah. What is it with certain Afghan men that they do things like this? Every time I think it's the end, then it's not. I think all the violence and depravity is men against women. But no, it can be male on male. It's simply depravity. Does jealousy play into it because Asadullah is handsome and smart? Whatever it is, it's just horrible. Years later, he is still traumatized and fearful of everyone except his closest family.

A couple of days later, the family got a call from the hospital that Asadullah was there and in a coma. The next day, he came out of the coma. It turned out that the rapists pistol-whipped him till he was unconscious. Nasima sent Maryam a picture of the teacher. Maryam said it looked like he had the same arrogance as the "rape guy," and Jennifer told Maryam to delete the picture. "You don't need to have that popping up on your phone or in your mind." This stuff will just tear your guts out. A couple of days later, local TV put Asadullah's picture on the news. This is very bad because it will incite anyone to come and beat up Asadullah for the reason that Asadullah brought dishonor to his family. Apparently, dishonoring the family works the same for both females *and males!* This is our first time with this variation of dishonor. This was serious enough that the family considered getting him out of Afghanistan for his safety.

The next day, Maryam called, crying hard. Sobbing, she says, "They beat up Asadullah and my cousin Ismail." Many of the family were staying some days in the hospital with Asadullah and were tired. Ismail said he would stay. Late that evening, some guys came in and beat up both Asadullah and Ismail. In addition to beating them up with their fists, they kicked each of them in the testicles. These were the rapists who wanted to let the family know who was in control. Maryam was beside herself, wallowing in pain and grief. I was thinking the depravity just won't stop. The family started to collect money to fly Asadullah and Ismail to Kabul and then to safety in India. Ismail had an aunt there with whom they could stay. A cousin living in Istanbul sent $500 and Maryam $500. But first, Asadullah and Ibrahim had to get treatment for scrotum injuries. After a couple of days, the family consensus was things had calmed down enough that they could cancel the trip and stay in Kunduz.

More Taliban atrocity

In October, Shir, another cousin of Maryam, disappeared, and the Taliban was the only one to suspect. Sure enough, they dumped him off at some distance from the house. "They beat him so bad…" Maryam said, gasping for air. "They beat him so bad. He has pain all over," but he had really bad pain in the leg that started with the botched operations some years ago. They just stomped on it. He also had a really huge pain in his back. And then, the worst, they sodomized him. Maryam said she couldn't even cry. Good god, more atrocity!

Where would this thing with the Taliban end?

In October, we were having dinner, and Maryam had an anxious look on her face. She said the Taliban killed one of her cousins and several of her family members. She said the cousin was twenty-two and had one child. Her husband had died earlier from something prior to the Taliban takeover. I inhaled and asked, "This is just piling more on top of all of what has happened to your family?" "Yes, Dad." "Where does this all go? Months, years? Until they shoot all of their enemies dead?" "Yes, Dad." Up until the Taliban takeover, things were getting better for Maryam's family back home and, in turn, for Maryam here in Canada. And then kaboom—the Taliban takes over. I just break down and sob, the first time since this Taliban stuff started. I was all about taking care of the business of getting

Aisha and Ali out. This short conversation just broke through my wall of maintaining emotionally, which shielded me unconsciously. And for Maryam, the Taliban takeover really took her down. Prior to their takeover, Maryam's counseling was working, psychiatric treatment and medications were working. Not perfect, but relatively stable. Then *kaboom! The Taliban takes over.*

After a counseling session, Maryam, Jennifer, and I went to lunch at McDonalds, and as is often after counseling sessions, Maryam told us what happened in the session. Maryam said her counselor pointed out that Maryam should work on having positive thought images, focus on fun and light movies, having pleasurable recreation, and so forth to counter the negative images causing the anxiety. Avoid talking about those bad images, not to suppress them but to replace them. It was bad enough before the Taliban. I said to Jennifer, "I don't think Maryam will hurt herself. But trying to lift this enormous weight off will not be easy."

On November 12th, somebody leaked the information that Aisha and Ali were Christians and it got to the Taliban. They stormed into the house, terrorizing everyone. Aisha and Ali were already in the cellar. When the two heard the Taliban come into the house, they jumped into the piles of garbage down there. "Stinky, rotten garbage," as Maryam explained. The Taliban came down to the cellar, but I guess they weren't smart enough to look in the garbage bins.

Passports and visas

Ali worked tirelessly and sometimes at his own peril to get passports for Aisha and himself. They finally got them October 23rd and immediately applied for visas to Tajikistan. Those are supposed to be in hand on Sunday, October 31. Once those are in hand, they will immediately get plane tickets to Tajikistan and fly out of the very real danger of remaining in Afghanistan. Even after weeks of an official of the Tajik Embassy telling them they could get a visa, suddenly the message changed—no visas for Afghans wanting to go to Tajikistan. Ali made a quick check and found out there were no visas available to five other Central Asian republics. In addition, Maryam said Arabic-Muslim countries are not good because of serious cultural discrimination.

November 17th, 2021, our two arrived in Pakistan

In an act of desperation to flee from the Taliban, Ali and Aisha decided to go to Pakistan because they could get visas in a few days and onto quick safety. On November 17, they flew to Islamabad, Pakistan. While it was definitely better than Afghanistan, Pakistan was still a foreign country with a foreign language and no family. Islamabad was a large city which is much more anonymous than Kunduz, making it more difficult to navigate. Ali, who speaks some English, is usually quiet during our WhatsApp calls, says Pakistanis have a "bad culture" and they don't like Afghans. In Afghanistan, the Taliban kills Tajiks (the country of their national origin), and in Pakistan, they just discriminate against Afghans. Pick your poison. And by the way, Zalika went with the two. The thought of having her two youngest grandchildren in another country was apparently too much. All of that said, it was a big day to get freedom from the Taliban and much to be thankful for. Their visas to Pakistan were good for 60 days plus an automatic fifteen-day extension.

The apartment they found was really bad—no carpet, no furniture, no heat. It was late November and very cold outside. They were using a space heater, and I warned them, "It's not safe, it's not safe!" I kept telling them to find a better place and that I was willing to pay the extra rent. Finally, they had bought a carpet and blankets to at least keep somewhat warm. After a couple of weeks, the space heater set the carpet on fire! The next day they got a better, safer apartment with a permanent, metal steam radiator for heat. Thank heavens!

About the time our three went for Pakistan, the attorneys in Canada advised going to India was a favorable opportunity. They said that India had an open door for Afghans, the cost is low, and the visa is good for a hundred and eighty days. The problem is that there are about forty thousand Afghans in line, and it could take months. Ali had considered it, but they wanted to get out very quickly. After they were in Pakistan for a while, I thought, just get your application into India and see what happens. So they went to the Indian Embassy in person, and the officials said that they do not accept applications from Pakistanis or anyone in Pakistan, regardless of their nationality. They would have to return to Afghanistan and apply from there, and, repeating what the attorneys had said, there are forty thousand Afghans in line. For these reasons, India became a no go. I had received an email from Women for Afghan Women, an advocacy group, in September with pages of many different ways to help Afghans in the new, repressive Taliban era, which included a list of twenty countries which were the best options for visas for Afghans seeking escape Afghanistan. It said that Brazil pretty much had an open-door policy. I spent almost a week putting the applications for visas together for the two for Brazil. As of December 14th, 2021, we were waiting for an appointment.

January 17th, 2022, our two returned to Afghanistan

On January 17th, 2022, sixty days after arrival in Pakistan, they returned to Afghanistan. Our two young Afghans and Zalika landed in a small town to the northwest of Kunduz across the border between Afghanistan and Tajikistan. One brother-in-law, who had a terrible reputation for irresponsibility, was supposed to pick them up and take them to a hotel where he had reserved a room. Why they picked him, I'll never know. When Maryam and I heard that, we thought that doesn't sound like a good idea to make him responsible to do anything. He's just not a very reliable guy. Sure enough, he was a no show. They called Ismail about 11:00 pm, and he drove up and picked them up and drove back to a nice hotel for $15 a night. Amazing. Hospital rooms are $200 a day, so the hotel is a good deal. They didn't want to stay with Zalika and Hussien, because they feared one of their neighbors might turn Ali and Aisha into the Taliban because they are Christians.

All of this time, our two have been living in a constant state of terror. Even in Pakistan they have been holed up in an apartment, still fearing the thought of having to return to Afghanistan if they don't get a more permanent visa to the Canada or some third country. And now here they were—back in Afghanistan. Maryam, Jennifer, and I agreed we shouldn't talk about these things; they just infected our minds, but it's hard not to.

In the middle of the night, Ali heard a noise in the hall and stepped out to see what was going on. The Taliban was sodomizing a young man in gang fashion. The Taliban hasn't given up!

The three stayed in the hotel room almost all of the time to avoid the Taliban, who seemed to be everywhere. They ordered most of their meals from the hotel and delivered to their room. Ismail went outside to pick up some food, and the Taliban beat him up because his hair was cut too short. Aisha has been crying a lot because of fear for over half a year of being accosted by scary men in Islamabad or the Taliban in Afghanistan. She and Ali decided to go meet with their counselor, but the Taliban stopped them and asked where their father and mother were, and they actually called Ismail and Nasima to verify how they were related. When you think about it, everybody in Afghanistan should be in collective group therapy.

Something missing in media coverage

I am a news junkie, and for eight years, I have paid special attention to news about Afghanistan. I read newspapers (the *Washington Post* and *New York Times*), listen to the radio news (NPR and BBC), and watch TV news (MSNBC, NBC, CBS, and ABC). I have also read numerous books about current events and the history of Afghanistan. It seems to me that there is something missing from the media, namely atrocities the Taliban has committed, such as those suffered by Maryam's family. Since the Taliban took over, the media regularly covers what the top echelons of Taliban leaders are saying about limiting girls' participation in school, etc., but not down-on-the-ground information about atrocities. I sent a letter to the editor of the *New York Times* and the *Washington Post*, two of the best investigative newspapers in the country, explaining the atrocities on Maryam's family. I heard nothing in response to either of my letters. I told our two about this in a WhatsApp call. Aisha said she had a schoolmate who was out walking with her mother, and the Taliban beat them up and then kidnapped her schoolmate, and this is 6 months after the August takeover. Maryam explained her thought that the Taliban has not let the Western media see these atrocities taking place, which sounds very plausible.

Uzbekistan... maybe

In October 2021, Uzbekistan was not accepting visa applications from Afghans, but by January 2022, they were. Soon after the three returned to Afghanistan, Ali made visa applications for himself and Aisha. Uzbekistan had several positive conditions, making it attractive. The visas were good for one year with the possibility of extension, and they could work. They had a relative who had arranged for Ali to work fixing cars, his specialty. The cost of housing was relatively low. Generally Uzbeks have liberal Muslim customs compared to the barbaric Taliban customs, but then that's not a difficult standard to meet. Women can go out freely without a male escort and without a hijab. Uzbeks are relatively tolerant of non-Muslim faiths, so Ali and Aisha would be able to freely practice their Christian faith. There is an Afghan community where they can speak Farsi, where they find out about work, generally socialize more easily, and live in their native culture, food, clothes, etc. Uzbekistan is far better than Afghanistan.

However, Ali and Aisha strongly would rather be in Canada. It is much safer, and they would have their sister whom they hadn't seen for seven years.

As of February 14, 2022, their application was pending. The Uzbek visa official kept telling them, "It will be Monday," and Monday comes, and he says, "Thursday" and it keeps getting pushed forward in the calendar to some indefinite date. The Taliban had been harassing and threatening the two, so they were strongly thinking of returning to Pakistan rather than waiting in Uzbekistan.

Ali had been working with an Afghan middleman to get visas to Uzbekistan. The Taliban found out what this guy was doing. In front of Kunduz's main mosque, a most revered, sacred, and ancient Muslim shrine, *the Taliban set the middleman on fire*—I repeat, *the Taliban set him on fire!!!* When a guy you've been doing business with gets set on fire, it stops you dead in your tracks and scares you to death. One degree of separation was too close. When Ali found this out, he just broke down crying. Maryam says she never saw him cry before, even when the Taliban brutalized him. When they brutalize you, you could give yourself 50/50 chance of surviving. When they set you on fire, it's hundred percent that you're gone. At the same time, the Taliban also set two other men on fire who are doing the same kind of business. The Taliban were obviously sending a message to anyone who might think of doing the same thing. (A similar method of punishment is that they cut the hand off of a robber. Primitive but no doubt effective.)

On a WhatsApp call on February 17th, I asked if India is a possibility. Ali said India stopped accepting Afghans. Another door closed.

We talked several times a week with Maryam, Aisha, and Ali

We talked with the two a couple of times a week, with Maryam translating. We saw their shining faces, sometimes Ali's desperate pleas about which county was a possibility. Nearly every call, they would ask, "Have you talked to the lawyers?" They actually meant, "Where are our visas to theCanada?" It tore our hearts out. These are real people, real lives. They are the real lives we have been trying to save. Their trauma and fear rippled to Maryam, Jennifer, and me. Jennifer had over hundred people in a prayer chain, praying for their safety. I told many of my family and friends, and many regularly ask about their welfare. Are they safe? Most Canadians don't have this kind of thing in their lives, so describing the terror of our two kids chills their bones.

Back to Pakistan

After the middleman was killed, Ali made the applications directly to the Uzbekistan Embassy in Kabul. But the Embassy said it would be Monday, then Thursday, and the day keeps getting pushed forward—same song, different singer. So Ali started making applications to Pakistan. But then the Taliban came upon the two plus their mother Zalika. They asked what about Aisha and said they could take her to keep her "safe." Zalika pleaded and cried and wailed and eventually passed out. Aisha was screaming, and Ali was yelling. After an hour, Ali, being pragmatic businessman, paid the Taliban a bribe, and they went away. On the same day, an "official" at the Pakistan Embassy demanded a $1,000 bribe. Ali argued but to no avail.

For over two weeks, we had very limited WhatsApp time with them. We finally made contact, and Ali whispered briefly from a closet that they feared the Taliban had been listening outside the door and that they feared the Taliban might bust in and hurt them because they were talking on the phone. Ali said he would explain what was going on once they got to Pakistan. Last week, we read in the paper that the Taliban was terminating evacuation flights. We and Ali misread it and thought they were terminating *all* flights. I reread the article and realized it was only evacuation flights, mostly with interpreters who had worked for the U.S. Department of Defense. Correct information and facts are extremely important, and anxiety can lead to misreads and wrong decisions.

We had kept our pastor up to date with Maryam and our two. I told him they tried a whole bunch of other countries, and Pakistan was the best choice. He had been on many church missions to third-world countries. Being a plain and direct-spoken guy, he said, "Well, if your best choice is Pakistan, you're in a world of hurt."

After what seemed like an eternity (it was actually about 7 weeks), on March 9th, the two flew back to Pakistan. They told me the visas were good for a year, and they could work. Ali looked in earnest for work, but it was hard because he spoke no Urdu, and a lot of Pakistanis don't like Afghans. Ali found a job washing dishes—for a $100 a month, and rent was $1,000 a month. I sent more money.

Frayed nerves and PTSD

Noor is Zalika's grandson, and he was losing a lot of weight, so they took him to the doctor, who said that he needed to go to Pakistan or India for specialists. Zalika took him to Islamabad and joined up with her two kids. The doctor said Noor had leukemia. I started thinking about exorbitant costs of radiation treatments. Friends told me about a St. Jude's program where they fly any kid in need from any part of the world and do the treatments—all for free. However, it turned out that the doctors in Islamabad wanted to treat him with medication. He took pills and drops three times a day for sixty days for $500, which is a lot less than the radiation treatments in Canada. Within a few days, he regained his appetite, started eating normal amounts of food, and gained weight. Thank heavens.

So now there were four of them in a two-room apartment, getting closer to a regular Afghan family. March turned to April, and April turned to May. They had been on the run from the Taliban from August 2021 to May 2022—a total of nine months. The four of them spent nearly all of their time in these two rooms. It's a wonder their nerves hadn't frayed before.

Applications for humanitarian visas denied

May 26th, 2022, the Canadian CIS sent a denial of applications for humanitarian parole visas to Ali and Aisha. It was a very, very sad day and a huge letdown. Our attorneys and many other immigration attorneys picked the humanitarian visa on purpose, or else they would not have spent their valuable time preparing them. But the CIS had a different opinion and denied nearly ninety-nine percent of thirty-five thousand applications. We weren't alone. It was amazing that Ali and Aisha were Christians in a Taliban-controlled country who would be punished by killing for a lesser reason—and they still didn't receive the visas. If Ali and Aisha don't qualify because they are Christians, who the heck does?! We had high hopes for the humanitarian visas but to no avail. However, we can't afford to dwell on a door that is closed. None of us. We had to look forward to the next possible open door.

Start in Western Hemisphere, going north to south

Jennifer had a flash of geographic brilliance. What is the geographic optimum way to go? Start with the Western Hemisphere, pick the country closest to Canada, and work southward, the goal being to get them to a country as close as possible to us. So we started with the U.S., and quickly, we found out that was a no go. Then onto Mexico and ran the search engine for "visas." Wow, Mexico had an asylum program, full-fledged! Go, go. Dig, dig for more details about the program. I called my friend, who lived in Mexico for about five years, married a Mexican national, and quizzed him on safety from gangs. He advised staying out of places where bad people hung out and do bad things, not just by region but by parts of cities. He described Cancun on the Yucatan Peninsula where he had lived a few years. After analyzing the options, it turns out you have to go to the Mexican Embassy *in the country where you are.* Damn… there was no Mexican Embassy or consulate in Pakistan since 2010. *A week down the tubes!* Moving along southward. Belize, no embassy in Pakistan. Costa Rica, the same, and furthermore no asylum program. Cuba, it seemed like they don't have restrictions on particular nationalities but were vague about letting any nationality in. And then four more Latin American countries were a no-go for one reason or another.

Then Ali said, Brazil!

Jennifer and I think, at least, it's in the Western Hemisphere! Obviously, Ali is gaining a grasp of world geography. However, Brazil costs a lot.

An official at the Brazilian Embassy in Islamabad explained that they could apply for a visa to Brazil that would allow permanent asylum. They could call for an appointment and get one the following week. Ali would get his appointment July 4th, Aisha on July 11th. Receipt of the visa would be three to four weeks after the appointment, making it August 25 for Ali. Ali got a call from the Brazilian Embassy on July 11th, a week after his interview, and they said they had approved his visa, but they didn't actually give him the visa. They wanted a lot of money $7,000 a piece!! That was outrageous—but anything to get them out of Afghanistan!

Aisha needed to get a revised passport so that her last name would be the same as his. For some unknown reason, it wasn't done that way in the first place. So the plan was for her to return to Afghanistan on June 25th, get the passport name changed, and return to Islamabad in time to make the application for her visa with the Brazilian Embassy on July 10th and the interview on July 11th. That would keep the schedule of getting these visas to Brazil as fast as possible.

I told Ali to ask Afghans in Pakistan what they had heard from Afghans who were in Brazil. Fourteen thousand dollars is a lot of money, and I wanted to know what the future holds in Brazil. Would it be like magic where now you're in Brazil and then poof—opportunity turns to disaster!

1. What did people do for housing when they first arrived in Brazil?
2. Had Afghans been really able to find jobs?
3. Had they found jobs where they earned enough to pay for rent, food, and basic expenses?
4. Had they been able to find housing they could afford?
5. Had there been a rise in prices in general? Food? Rent?
6. Had the Afghans stayed in Sao Paulo?
7. What other cities did they go to?
8. Did any go to Brasilia, the capital and a much smaller city than Sao Paulo or Rio de Janeiro?
9. Was there a particular city or place within a city where Afghans have settled?
10. Did Afghans help each other out in finding housing and other things to get settled?

After getting to Brazil, they would go to a refugee camp near Sao Paulo for two months to learn basic survival Portuguese, get some kind of job training, and generally get oriented to Brazil. Later, Maryam told us that the process would take four months. Many Afghans had spent their four months there, and some were still there in the "camp", whatever that meant. Ali had talked with Afghans in Islamabad who had relatives there from whom he had learned all of this. He verified the visas were for permanent asylum. The plan was that once they spent the four months in the camp, then they could leave the camp, go to some place "on the economy," and find jobs with pay that would be enough to cover the basic needs for the three: rent, food, and clothes.

Ali told us he had been going to the Brazilian Embassy for many days, talking to this official there about these visas. On July 7th, Ali went, and the official said they would have to start paying and that they had to put down on the counter $7,000 for Ali's visa versus a fraction that was agreed to before. Ali was taken aback and asked where the visa was. The guy said it would come soon. Ali argued him down by fifty percent ($3,500!) and actually handed the money over. The guy said, "You'll be lucky to get out of the airport in Sao Paulo," meaning this was all illegal. *Boom, crash!! This guy was a shyster, a liar!* He was not a real official who issued legal visas. And he was a Pakistani on top of it. *Ali was so very embarrassed*, and he just couldn't talk with us for a long time. I told Maryam, please tell him. I knew he was doing his best. Please tell him.

Checked out visas to twenty countries

To recap, back in the beginning, when the Taliban came to town and committed atrocities on 14 members of her family, Jennifer and I felt compelled to get Aisha and Ali out of Afghanistan as soon as possible—it was a matter of literal life and death. After the attorneys filed the applications for the humanitarian visas to the Canada, nearly every time we were on our calls with them they would ask, "How these applications were coming along?" They would say, "Ask the attorneys…did you ask the attorneys?" And we would have to reply, every time, that a federal government agency is reviewing the applications and neither we nor the attorneys can make it go faster. It was just heart-breaking to have to go through that and look them in the face on WhatsApp. The string of atrocities on their family palpably drove their anxiety.

At one point, we sent a letter to the President and our elected officials. In response to that letter, we eventually got a phone call from a representative of CIS, who I must say, had a snarly tone. That followed with a letter that effectively said we just had to wait for the agency to complete its review. We have come to find out that there are many types of visas to get into Canada.

Here is a summary of our efforts on those visas.

- August 1st, 2021. Turkey, $2,300 per person, but we spent no money. We investigated, and then Turkey changed policy: no visas for Afghans.
- August 15th. India, $1,800 per person, but we spent no money. There were long waits because they had over 40,000 applicants, so India was a no go. They had to get out quickly.
- September 7. Canada. The law firm paid the $575 application fee for Aisha and filed the application for the humanitarian parole visa.
- October 28th, Canada. The law firm paid the $575 application fee for Ali and filed the application.
- October and November for several weeks. Ali investigated Tajikistan for a couple of weeks, and then Tajikistan stopped accepting visa applications from Afghans.
- Ali investigated five other Central Asian countries, and none was accepting visa applications from Afghans.
- November. Pakistan, $500 per person. The three got their visas and arrived in Pakistan on November 17th. Those visas took only three days and which they took

because they needed to get out of Afghanistan as soon as possible. The visas were good for 60 days plus two fifteen-day extensions.

- Later in November, the attorneys advised India, but there were forty-thousand Afghans who had applied, and it was going to take a while. Fees turned out to be in the order of $100 versus $1,800 per person we had understood in August.

- January 18, 2023. Uzbekistan, $2,000 per person for a one-year visa. A long, ugly story unravels with the Taliban burning up the middleman and ending with Uzbekistan stopping the issuance of visas to Afghans.

- January and February, I investigated Mexico, Belize, Costa Rica, Cuba, and four more Latin American countries. Each had reasons that made applications a no-go.

- July 7th, Brazil, $5,500 per person. Forked over $3,500 for one application, then found out it was a guy scamming. Better than $5,500 x 2.

- That's a grand total of twenty countries—the door is closed to legal, long-term (over a year) visa applications. Canada isn't the only one with a door closed.

Zalika had returned to Afghanistan in May after Noor had gotten his medical treatments, and in late June, Aisha had gone back to Afghanistan to get the new passport with the name change. Whereupon, and once again, Zalika proceeded to attempt to arrange yet another marriage with an Afghan guy in London, a high bidder as usual. At this point, Zalika, Hussein, Ali, Aisha, Ismail, Nasima, Noor, and Rabela were under one roof in Kunduz. One day, there was a "knock-knock" at the door (as Maryam refers to someone knocking at the door). Ismail was not sure who that might be. Virtually all of the family and friends who come to the door just walk in, they don't knock-knock. Ismail, wondered who this might be, opened the door, and there were four women.

"Uh, who are you?" Ismail asked.

"Well, we're friends of Hazrat," one of these four women replied. Ismail was wondering, "What is going on?", but he let them in.

"We are here to arrange the marriage of our brother with Aisha. He is twenty-five, quite handsome, and wealthy. We are his sisters," the one sister said.

One handed a picture of him on her phone. Ismail looked at it and looks a lot more like forty and ugly—money can't make up for those two strikes. Plus, the fundamental factor—Aisha is not up for sale. Ismail was furious. Once again, he grabbed Aisha by the hand, quickly ran out of the house, went to a place where Zalika couldn't find them. In this case, it was one of his cousins. He and Sarya stayed there a couple of nights until he could find a new apartment, and then he got Nasima, Noor, and Rabela to bring them to the new apartment.

A week later, Maryam called Jennifer and me up with the daily news from Afghanistan and Pakistan and was upset but in a way somewhat different than the "normal." "Ismail is in the hospital, he got hurt in a traffic accident…" She heaves a sigh of distress. "Why is it that all of the time since Aisha has been in Pakistan, no accidents or traumas have happened to Ismail? But now Ismail took Aisha into hiding, and all of a sudden, Ismail got hurt in a traffic accident and landed in the hospital? I'll tell you why. Zalika had control of Aisha, tried to arrange a marriage, and sell her off, resulting in Ismail taking

Aisha off to yet another safe house so Zalika couldn't get her hands on Aisha. And then somehow, for some unknown reason, Ismail now ends up in a serious car accident." You might say Zalika is hard-wired to arrange marriages.

Abortion and atrocities

After the Taliban atrocities, Nasima had been beating her two children, then 6 and 4, and they have been hitting back. This didn't seem characteristic of her, so I asked Maryam when it started, was it after the Taliban raped her? Yes. So here were very lasting ramifications of the original atrocities. Also, she got pregnant from the rape and had an abortion. I would imagine this had its own form of trauma.

About the same time, I ran into a couple of women I didn't know well, and is often the case, it doesn't take long till I get over to some part of the Maryam story. This time, I got into the part where the Taliban committed atrocities on fourteen of Maryam's family. The one lady asks in some exasperation and just trying to grasp the horror of it all, "Is this just Maryam's family, or did the Taliban pick out her family for some particular reason?" This conversation was quite animated and intense, and I got a little frustrated that she didn't understand the context. I inhaled to void my frustration and said, "You see, the Taliban was rampaging and pillaging *everywhere*, going house to house and accosting people *at random*. If you weren't Taliban or ethnic Pashtun, you were the enemy! And these Taliban are a vicious people." Then she got it. Later, I had a conversation similar to this with a friend who is well travelled and well versed in world events and cultures. He said he was having trouble understanding the logic of these events. I told him, "There is no logic!"

Chapter 10: Good News! And The Other Shoe

One year on, living tentative peace with the Taliban

As of August 2023, Ali and Aisha had been back in Kunduz since August of 2022 for a whole year. In retrospect, by October 2022, the Taliban had stopped committing atrocities, at least on Maryam's family, with one exception I describe below. However, it's hard to say when the trauma will be resolved. The Taliban was not committing attacks, busting in houses, kidnapping, beating, hassling people on the streets, and the like. Day-to-day life had become peaceable enough. They weren't allowing girls to go to school beyond the sixth grade, including university level. They weren't allowing women to work for non-governmental organizations many of which provided food aid, protection, and counseling of women who had been raped or faced domestic abuse, economic assistance, and the like. This eliminated pay that would circulate in the economy, leaving those women without income. Poverty and food insecurity have become major problems since the Taliban takeover. These larger-scale problems were definitely not good for the larger society, but they weren't weighing so heavily on Maryam's family. This was with the exception food and education for Aisha. So things were bad in larger scale ways, but the Taliban were not committing atrocities. It's all relative.

We had been sending money to our three plus Ismail and his family for their rent, food, counseling, and medication for PTSD so they can keep the wolf from the door. Ali is the real financial savior. Before the Taliban he started repairing cars at age seventeen, using his outstanding mechanical aptitude and renting a garage. Then he started buying and selling cars and making enough money to support eight of his closest family members! Upon their return to Kunduz in August Ali tested the waters of starting the business back up, and it didn't work. He tried again in October, and he started getting it going again, gradually making more and more money. Amazing! And he started training Ismail how to repair cars so they would be able to support themselves. He was making more money and supporting the eight of his family he was before, meaning the less I have had to send money over. As long as this holds and as long as Maryam is able to work and support herself, the less I will have to transfer out of the monthly cash flow.

This is a long way from the two going on the run from the Taliban and Maryam fainting.

This is the good news—at last!!

Our Maryam-Jan

Here is an update to this is that in the eighth year since Maryam has been with us. The severe traumatic events back home and those with Maryam here in Canada have subsided—amazing! I hate to count on that stability too much because there are too many unknowns that could bring it all down, too much history to the contrary. And the wild card is that the Taliban is in charge. But for now, the past problems have abated. Maryam started working in a new department store and has been getting literally four and five times more customers to sign up for credit cards than any of her co-workers. She has such an outgoing personality, she just engages people, making them laugh, and all of a sudden, they are signing up for a credit card. She is very funny and makes anyone she is in contact with laugh. Many customers have even taken the time to email management to compliment her on her professionalism, good nature, and how good they feel after being with her. The store has given her awards, including "Employee of the Month". A district supervisor came to the local store, singled her out, and asked her what her secret was to get so many customers to sign up for credit cards. She answered, "That's my secret!" getting him to laugh. We think he figured out her secret.

Another factor is that we now live in a London, Ontario where there are essentially no Afghans. Her first three years with us, we lived in Toronto, with the second-highest population of Afghan Canadians in Canada, and many of her problems stemmed from fellow Afghans, sooner or later, abusing her. As Esmatullah said, "Don't trust Afghans, *not even me!*" There are, of course, non-Afghans who have caused problems for her, but not nearly what happened with the Afghans in Toronto, it would seem. Her life has been better in our new place.

Her resilience is phenomenal. Any one of these traumatic events I recount in this book could easily have resulted in very antisocial or criminal behavior or driven her to suicide. We realized her resilience even eight years ago and each ensuing year. Each new traumatic event would push her down, and then she'd pop back up. She acknowledges there will be bumps on the road in the future, but she says she feels equipped emotionally to take them on. She has gone from barely being able to keep her head above the ravaging sea to walking up on land away from the ocean.

Maryam tells me now, "Yeah, dad-jan, I feel pretty good."

The other shoe—somebody rats to the Taliban that Aisha and Ali are Christians

March 25th, Maryam called and unloaded the truth. Seven Taliban busted the door open and went into Ismail and Nasima's house and beat up all but one of them, badly enough that Ismail, Ali, and Aisha had to go to the hospital. This actually happened on March 20th, but Maryam was so overcome with grief it took her five days till she could talk without crying uncontrollably. Maryam said, "*Somebody ratted to the Taliban that Ali and Aisha are Christians.*" (See Appendix 4 about Christians in Afghanistan) Maryam explained further, "The Taliban asked where the Bible was and then burnt it." You see, this is a war of religion, which can be a bit hard to grasp. In Canada there are tensions over religious matters, but the Taliban is one of the most radical fringe elements of those who call themselves Muslims. There are so many radical things they do, so much so that centrist, mainline Muslims would not consider the Taliban to be Muslims. True Muslims would not commit the atrocities that they did on 14 of Maryam's family.

They told Nasima *they had not raped her because it was Ramadan, they just beat her up*. That's what you call grace. Maryam continues, Noor, was crying uncontrollably as he watched the Taliban beating Nasima. *Then, the Taliban beat up Noor. He is little boy, he is just six years old. Evil, evil, Satan!* Maryam and I hung up, and I just lost it, bawling uncontrollably.

Two days later, Aisha continued to cry uncontrollably. She was completely panic-stricken. She just couldn't get the images of the Taliban busting the door in and beating her and nearly everyone else. This is why she and Ali were on the run for a year. Nearly nine months back in Afghanistan, with no hassles from the Taliban, things were tolerable. Then *kaboom*. Aisha asked the doctor if she was still a virgin, fearing that perhaps she had passed out and the Taliban had raped her. Thank heavens the doctor said no. It's two weeks later, and all of those in the house when the Taliban busted in are still in a horrid state of shock. Our Maryam-Jan too.

How the Amish respond to a guy shooting 10 of their girls

I was just overcome with sadness anger, and rage. Then I thought about all of the gun violence in the U.S., decade after decade. Those survivors I think have every right to anger and rage. But then I remembered the event with Amish from a few years back. Here is what I found on Google.

October 2nd, 2006 in Lancaster County, Pennsylvania, local police, responding to a 911 call found 10 Amish girls ages 6-13 had been shot at school by Charles Roberts. The violence that is far too common in one society blasted its way into the non0violent, peaceful community of "the gentle people". Five of the girls died. Amish parents tried to console themselves by saying the five girls who had died were "safe in the arms of Jesus." The day after the shooting, 1,600 people gathered for a prayer service at one local church, while hundreds more met at other churches for prayer. I all, over four million dollars was raised in support of the families.

Charlie Roberts was a milk truck driver who serviced the local community, including the farms of some of the families. Nine years earlier his wife Amy gave birth to their first child, a baby girl. However, the baby died after living only 20 minutes. Apparently his daughter's death affected him greatly. He never forgave God for her death, and eventually planned to get revenge.

In the midst of their grief over this shocking loss, the Amish community didn't cast blame, they didn't point fingers, they didn't hold a press conference with attorneys at their sides. Instead, the Amish community reached out with grace and compassion toward the killer's family, The afternoon of the shooting an Amish grandfather of one of the girls who was killed expressed forgiveness toward the killer, Charles Roberts. That same day Amish neighbors visited the Roberts family to comfort them in their sorrow and pain. Later that week the Roberts family was invited to the funeral of one of the Amish girls who had been killed. Following the funeral at Charales Robert's funeral, Amish mourners outnumbered the non-Amish.

It's ironic that the killer was tormented for nine years by the pre-mature death of his young daughter and never forgave God for her death. Yet, after he cold-bloodedly shot 10 innocent Amish school girls, the Amish almost immediately forgave him and show compassion toward his family.

In a world at war and in a society that often points fingers and blames others, this reaction was unheard of. Many reporters and interested followers of the story asked, "How could they forgive such a terrible, unprovoked act of violence against innocent lives?"

The Amish culture closely follows the teachings of Jesus who taught his followers to forgive one another, to place the needs of others before themselves, and to rest in the knowledge that God is still in control and can bring good out of any situation. Love and compassion toward others is to be life's theme. Vengeances and revenge is to be left to God.[10]

If we all had this grace, we would have such a better world. But we have a way to go. I thought I had a happy ending to this book, but sadly, it is not so. The war between darkness and the light continues, and the human struggle goes on. So I will close it here so I can get it into print for distribution to as wide an audience as I can find, so maybe, just maybe, I can cast a little more light and inspire readers to cast some light, too.

Appendix 1

Violence against girls and women—the bigger picture

Introduction

Most of the documents cited below are from the asylum application for Maryam prepared by attorneys. I do not cite the names of the attorneys or the firm they worked for in order to protect their safety. The asylum application is about five hundred pages long, one hundred pages about Maryam as an individual, and four hundred pages of supporting documents which describe the Afghanistan country context. I have extracted the most pertinent parts of those documents and put them in the following without quotes. They are primarily from 2008 to 2014, not long before they prepared her asylum application. I have found other sources which supplement these other sources.

Summary: violence and abuse against women and girls in Afghanistan

- **Violence and abuse against women and girls is endemic to the society**

Violence against women and girls, including domestic violence, sexual harassment, and rape, is pervasive and endemic.

The violence that scars the lives of a huge proportion of Afghan women and girls is rooted in Afghan culture, customs, attitudes, and practices. Afghan women have limited freedom to escape the norms and traditions that dictate a subservient status for females. Afghanistan remains one of the poorest countries in the world. Structural violence is exacerbated by dire levels of poverty. While all indications are that this violence is pervasive, it is still underreported.[11]

According to a 2013 survey, 1,051 women suffered from different types of violence. These types of violence experienced by those women exceed 3,331 instances. There were a total of 889 instances of physical violence, 808 instances of verbal and psychological violence, 715 instances of economic violence, and 256 instances of sexual violence.[12]

Ninety percent of all reported cases of violence take place within the victim's own family, and the husbands take the first place. The figures for mental or psychological damage or emotional duress are distressing, as compared to other consequences such as physical disabilities.[13]

Afghanistan was the world's most dangerous country for women in 2011, according to a pool of two hundred and thirteen gender experts.[14]

Brutal forms of subjugation of women and girls are made possible by a commodified criminal economy, total lack of security, and the erosion of social bonds of trust and solidarity.[15]

Violence can be sexual, physical, psychological. Forced marriage is strongly related to other forms of violence and remains widespread and socially accepted. Forced marriages often include women and girls threatened with violence, kidnapped, or are traded through informal dispute mechanisms, such as to settle a rape case, often when they are fifteen or younger. One report found that of five hundred and fifty women surveyed, fifty nine percent were married against their will, and thirty-eight percent reported being married between the ages of eleven and fifteen years.[16]

Women and girls were subjected to systematic discrimination that, effectively, confined most females to their homes. Females were not permitted out in public unless accompanied by a mahram (a male relative who serves as chaperone).[17]

Women and girls often "run away" from the violence in their marriage and have long faced punishment from family and local governing bodies for leaving home without permission.[18]

Eighty percent of women face forced marriages, and fifty seven percent of girls are married before the legal marriage age of sixteen.[19]

The Law on Elimination of Violence Against Women, adopted in 2009, remains largely unenforced, according to a 2013 report.[20]

In 2013, a draft law prepared by Afghan government officials reintroduced execution by stoning [emphasis added] as the punishment for the "crime" of adultery. One observer was horrified but not that surprised. As of 2013, the barbaric practice of virginity tests continues.[21] Violence against women was at record levels in 2013.[22]

- **Rape**

Rape is an ugly crime and an everyday occurrence in all parts of the country. It is a human rights problem of profound proportions. The issue of "honour" is a socio-cultural norm that is central to rape and efforts to counter its prevalence. Shame is attached to rape rather than to the perpetrator.[23]

Preliminary data in 2009 suggests that rape is a widespread occurrence in all parts of Afghanistan and in all communities and all social groups. The majority of rape cases that have been reported involve young girls (as young as three years old). Many perpetrators of rape are close family members of the victim, or otherwise known to the victim.[24]

Private feuds, such as those between families or within communities, are also a motive for sexual violence. In such contexts, rape is used to "dishonour" another family, tribe or clan, to obtain revenge for a previous crime.[25]

Rape victims are more stigmatized than the rapists.[26]

Soviet soldiers raped women.27Taliban committed gang rapes in 2015.[27]

- **Husbands and other male relatives are the main abusers**

Husbands, by far, are the main abusers, or seventy percent of those surveyed.[28] [Source 14, page 22] However, another source indicates that the husband was the main abuser for thirty-one percent of women, while the mother-in-law was the perpetrator for twenty-four percent of women.[29] [The wide difference in the numbers is probably due to the difficulties in collecting such data. However, each study has a large sample size, 4,700 and 1,051, respectively.]

- **Self-immolation**

The burn unit of Herat Hospital admitted a record number of women who had attempted to set themselves on fire in 2012.[30]

• **After the Taliban takeover in 2021**

The U.S. State Department reports a lack of investigation of and accountability for gender-based violence in 2021, both before and after the takeover of the Taliban.[31]

The despair created by the loss of gains women and girls had made in Afghanistan before 2021 is devastating, says an Afghan-Canadian women's organization.[32]

Since the Taliban took power in August 2021, the human rights situation of women and girls in Afghanistan has deteriorated, leading to the situation that "women are erased." The Taliban have deprived women and girls of their human rights, removed women from spheres of public life, and undone women's agency, according to authoritative sources.[33]

Many case stories of individual women and girls are cited throughout these documents to illustrate points made about conditions in the broader population, with diverse sources corroborating each other.

1. Living with violence, 2008

The Survey Population

A survey on domestic violence was conducted on women in 4,700 households located in 16 provinces throughout

Afghanistan. Considerable effort was made to ensure that the sample of women reflected the geographic, ethnic, linguistic, and cultural diversity of Afghan women. Within the provinces, women were interviewed from rural and urban communities. Women from different ethnic communities were also surveyed in proportion to the ethnicities living in the province. Members of the Kochi community, a traditionally nomadic group, were also interviewed in settlements in and around Kabul. [In other words, the survey was intended to be representative of the whole population of Afghans.]

Marriage Context

Almost all (ninety-six percent) of the women were married. Three percent were widowed, and one percent were divorced. In ninety-one percent of marriages, the husband and wife were from the same ethnic background. Thirteen percent of women were in polygamous marriages: ten percent of all women were in marriages that involved one other wife; two percent involved two other wives; 0.5 percent had three other wives; 0.1 percent had four other wives; and 0.1 percent had five other wives or more. In eighty-seven percent of cases, the first wife was interviewed for this survey. Only twenty-six percent of respondents knew their husbands well before they were married, while twenty-seven percent knew them a little, and forty-seven percent did not know their husbands at all prior to their marriage.

Family Context

Many respondents (fifty-two percent) were living in large families of six to ten members, and twenty-four percent lived in families of ten people or more: Ten percent of respondents had no children; twenty-two percent had one or two children; thirty percent had three-four children; Thirty percent had five to seven children; eight percent had eight to ten children, and one percent had more than ten children. A variety of age groups were included in the survey with women ranging in age from between ten to fourteen years (one percent) to over fifty years. Nearly all respondents were married to men older than themselves, with variations in the age differences.

The Pervasiveness of Violence

An overwhelming majority of women, eighty-seven percent, reported experiencing at least one form of domestic violence (physical, sexual, psychological, or forced marriage), and most (sixty-two percent) experienced multiple forms of violence. A seventeen percent of the women had experienced sexual violence, with eleven percent of women experiencing rape, one percent experiencing injury to their sexual organs, and five percent being denied sexual intercourse by their husband.

> - Over half of the women, fifty-two percent, had experienced physical violence. A thirty-nine percent said they had been hit by their husband in the last year.
> - A seventy-four percent of the women experienced psychological violence, including threats, social, economic, and cultural violence, and verbal violence.

- One quarter of the women received threats of a beating from their husbands, four percent were threatened with divorce, and three percent were threatened by their husband that he would take another wife. Five percent of women received threats of death from their husband.

- Forty one percent of the women were prevented from participating in public or social life with thirty-two percent being prevented from visiting friends or relatives or participating in public ceremonies or gatherings. Eighteen percent of women were prevented from spending money. Forty-nine percent of the women were prevented from engaging in cultural and religious activities, and of those, thirty percent were prevented from participating in religious affairs or visiting shrines.

- A fifty-six percent of women reported experiencing verbal abuse, including insulting and taunting.

Forced and Child Marriage

A fifty-nine percent of the women were in forced marriages. There were wide variations by province, ranging from a low of twenty-one percent in Daikundi to a high of ninety-two percent in Khost, where almost every marriage was forced. Forced marriage was strongly related to other forms of violence: sixty-four percent of women who were forced to marry reported experiencing physical violence, compared to thirty-seven percent of the women who married freely; eighty percent forced to marry reported psychological violence compared to sixty-six percent in free marriages; and twenty-two percent in forced marriages reported sexual violence, compared to eleven percent in marriages freely entered into.

Girls aged ten to fourteen were more likely to experience all forms of violence than girls and women fifteen years of age and older. In particular, thirty-three percent of girls in this age group reported sexual violence, which was almost double the incidence for females aged fifteen years and older. However, the thirty-three percent of girls between the ages of ten and fourteen who reported sexual violence is comprised of only thirteen girls. A sixty-three percent reported physical violence compared to fifty-two percent for older girls and women.

The Perpetrators of Violence

The husband was the main abuser for thirty-one percent of women, while the mother-in-law was the perpetrator for twenty-four percent of women. Other family members responsible for abuse included the sister-in-law (ten percent), brother-in-law (ten percent), father-in-law (seven percent), and the husband's uncle (two percent).[34]

2. Forced marriages in Afghanistan, 2008

Seventy to eighty percent of women face forced marriages in Afghanistan. A fifty-seven percent of girls are married before the legal marriage age of sixteen.[35]

3. Silence is violence: end the abuse of women in Afghanistan, 2009

Violence against women is deeply seated in the culture

Afghanistan is widely known and appreciated for its rich history, culture, literature, and arts, as well as its magnificent landscape. It is also widely known that large numbers of Afghanis die, or live wretched lives, because violence is an everyday fact of life. Such violence is not openly condoned, but neither is it challenged nor condemned by society-at-large or by state institutions.

Violence is pervasive throughout Afghanistan. It has diverse manifestations in different parts of the country. Violence against women is widespread and deeply rooted as well as acute. The violence that scars the lives of a huge proportion of Afghan women and girls is rooted in Afghan culture, customs, attitudes, and practices. Afghan women have limited freedom to escape the norms and traditions that dictate a subservient status for females…Violence, in its acute form, makes its presence felt in widespread lawlessness and criminality. All these forms of violence are closely linked to a deeply entrenched culture of impunity that is, in part, an outcome of decades of conflict and indifference to a justice agenda that would also allow for a transition from, and draw a line under, a long history of egregious human rights violations.

Rape and "honour"

On the issue of rape, UNAMA's [United Nations Assistance Mission in Afghanistan] research found that although under-reported and concealed, this ugly crime is an everyday occurrence in all parts of the country. It is a human rights problem of profound proportions. Women and girls are at risk of rape in their homes and in their communities, in detention facilities, and as a result of traditional harmful practices to resolve feuds within the family or community.

The issue of "honour" is a socio-cultural norm that is central to the issue of rape and efforts to counter its prevalence. Shame is attached to the rape victim rather than to the perpetrator. Victims often find themselves being prosecuted for the offence of zina (adultery) and are denied access to justice. The problem is compounded when communities subject female victims to lifelong stigma and shame. Moreover, society may call for, or condone, sexual violence through harmful traditional practices such as baad (the practice of handing over girls to settle disputes), or by insisting that a victim marry the rapist.

Women and girls are suppressed

Women and girls were subjected to systematic discrimination that, effectively, confined most females to their homes. Females were not permitted out in public unless accompanied by a mahram (a male relative who serves as chaperone).

The contemporary situation of Afghan women is shaped by harmful traditional practices, many of which preceded Islam. Such practices and related perspectives contradict the fundamental tenets of Islam but have served to suppress women, restrict their movements outside the home, leave them vulnerable in the face of violence, and violate their basic human rights. Decades of armed conflict, coupled with political turmoil, widespread impunity, and limited access to formal, effective, or credible justice systems, have been devastating for Afghans, women, and men. Insecurity, coupled with fears for personal safety, have been hugely detrimental, and hindered efforts geared to undoing deeply engrained discrimination that marginalize women…

Violence exacerbated by poverty

While an enormous amount of resources has been poured into Afghanistan [from 2001 to 2021 during the period of occupation by allied forces], it remains one of the poorest countries in the world with alarming socio-economic indicators. Afghanistan is ranked 174th out of a hundred and seventy-eight countries… Structural violence, including the persistent marginalization of women, is exacerbated by dire levels of poverty. A range of factors inhibit effective, equitable, and sustainable development. The war, organized crime, impunity, and rampant lawlessness, particularly in conflict-affected areas, work against community development and, by extension, access to essential services, including health care and justice mechanisms. A forty percent of the country is not accessible to humanitarian aid workers for extended periods. This is particularly worrying in a setting where 6.6 million people do not meet their minimum food requirements and where almost half of the population is living below the poverty line.

The adult literacy rate for Afghans over fifteen years of age is twenty-eight percent, including thirteen percent for females. In rural areas where seventy-four percent of the Afghans reside, it is estimated that ninety percent of women cannot read or write. Research also reveals that forty-three percent of females are less than eighteen years old when they marry. Afghanistan has one of the worst maternal mortality rates in the world; one woman dies every twenty-seven minutes due to pregnancy-related complications. This amounts to around 25,000 deaths per annum. Indeed, while the average life expectancy is forty-four years, some twenty years short of the global average, women in Afghanistan die at a younger age than men, notwithstanding the high level of male casualties in armed conflict.

Other troubling trends include an apparent backlash against the empowerment of women and their participation in public life. There is inadequate investment in efforts needed to counter deeply engrained discrimination that effectively condemns the majority of Afghan women to feudal-like conditions [Page 8].

Indeed, for a huge swathe of Afghan society, and particularly women, the ability to enjoy rights, that are fundamental to the safety and dignity of human beings everywhere, is extremely limited… Human rights defenders and others who support the emancipation of Afghan women, face particularly daunting challenges given the history, culture, and prevailing perspectives surrounding the role of females in Afghan society.

Socio-cultural barriers and traditional practices

One of the major barriers to realizing women's rights in Afghanistan is the way in which traditional practices and conservative interpretations of social norms restrict women's participation in public life. Traditions are often reinforced by arbitrary invocation of religion to further restrict women's movement.

Harmful traditional practices, in some cases preceding Islam, have been reinforced by tribal, community, and religious leaders in the name of religion. The concept of "tradition" has, however, to be treated with a degree of caution as, "What to Western eyes looks like tradition is in many instances, the manifestation of new and more brutal forms of subjugation of the weak, made possible by a commodified criminal economy, total lack of security, and the erosion of bonds of trust and solidarity that were tested to the limit by war, social upheaval, and poverty." [Deniz Kandiyoti, Old Dilemmas or New Challenges? The Politics of Gender and Reconstruction in Afghanistan, Development and Change, Vol. 38, no 2, 2007, pp. 169-199.]

As a result, many communities and families sincerely believe that women should stay at home. A popular Afghan saying encapsulates this: "Women are made for homes or the graves." The tradition of segregation of the sexes reinforces this belief.

Rape

Afghan society perceives women to be the guardians of culture and the custodians of a family's "honour." As a result, women are seen as "dishonouring" their families and communities when they are subjected to sexual violence. As such, it is the girl or woman—the rape victim—and not the perpetrator who carries the shame of the crime. As Afghan families customarily wish to uphold their "honour" by hiding incidents of rape of family members, the extent of the problem of rape within Afghan society remains unknown. In the interest of preserving "honour," and preventing ostracism and humiliation, Afghan women are under a lot of pressure to remain silent.

Sexual violence is under-reported in Afghanistan. However, available information points to a widespread phenomenon. It affects all communities and all segments of the population.

More should be done by the Government to promote change in societal attitudes and practices that at Times condone sexual violence through harmful customs such as baad—the handing over of a girl as "compensation" to settle a dispute or a crime—or insisting that a victim marry her rapist.

When is rape reported? In general, Afghan women and men consider discussing issues related to sex and sexual violence as taboo, as women's sexuality is effectively controlled by men. In the course of this research, UNAMA found it extremely difficult to use terms like "rape," "sexual consent," and "zina [adultery]." The issue of marital rape is never considered or reported, since women have no choice in terms of consenting to sexual intercourse with their spouse [page 21].

Early and forced marriages are, in this respect, particularly conducive to marital rape, including of very young girls. The power imbalance in the relationship between men and women within the family means that husbands decide over issues related to their partners' sexuality, including the frequency and nature of sexual intercourse.

UNAMA's preliminary data gathering suggests that rape is a widespread occurrence in all parts of Afghanistan and in all communities, and all social groups.

The majority of rape cases that have been reported involve young girls (as young as three years old) or females aged between seven and thirty, with a fair number of cases ranging between ten and twenty years of age. Women are at risk in their homes and communities, and on the streets whilst travelling to and from work or school. A significant number of reported cases coincided with armed robberies and kidnapping, and several recorded cases involved gang-rape. Women in both rural and urban settings are at risk of rape, but the risk appears to be greater for women in rural areas. Unaccompanied women and those who have previously been subjected to sexual violence are at greater risk, as are widows, divorced women, and women whose husbands are out of the country. In the latter case, abuse, mainly involves beatings, but sometimes sexual violence by the husband's male relatives. Similarly, girls who run away from home, including from forced marriage, are also at risk as they are perceived as an easy target. Moreover, when it comes to sexual violence in the family, observers note that illiterate or poor women are less likely to report cases of violence, including rape.

Analysis of cases revealed that many perpetrators are close family members of the victim, or otherwise known to the victim. A large number of cases were of incest. In addition, a number of rape cases involving young women married to older men were committed by the husband's brothers or sons.

Private feuds, such as those between families or within communities are also a move [sic] for sexual violence. In such contexts, rape is used to "dishonour" another family, tribe or clan, to obtain revenge for a previous crime. Men thus enter into a cycle of revenge, based on sexual abuse of women. Sexual violence and rape are seen as 'compensating' for an earlier crime.[36]

Case example: avenging "honor"

In Farah province, a father referred the case of his young daughter who was having a 'liaison' with a neighbour to a local Jirga [an assembly of leaders that makes decisions by consensus]. Elders decreed that the man having an affair should give money, his younger sister, and his six-month-old baby daughter to the girl's father as compensation. Members of the girl's family, however, allegedly abducted and raped one of the nieces of this man to avenge their "honour."[37]

4. Afghanistan is the world's most dangerous country for women, 2011

Violence, dismal healthcare, and brutal poverty make Afghanistan the world's most dangerous country for women… a Thomson Reuters Foundation expert poll said….the global survey of perceptions of threats [consider] factors ranging from domestic abuse and economic discrimination to female foeticide [abortion of a fetus], genital mutilation and acid attacks.

Ongoing conflict, NATO airstrikes, and cultural practices combine to make Afghanistan a very dangerous place for women… Trust Law asked two hundred and thirteen gender experts from five continents to rank countries by overall perceptions of danger as well as by six risks. The risks were health threats, sexual violence, non-sexual violence, cultural or religious factors, lack of access to resources, and trafficking. Afghanistan emerged as the most dangerous country for women overall and worst in three of the six risk categories: health, non-sexual violence, and lack of access to economic resources…

Poll respondents included aid professionals, academics, health workers, policymakers, journalists, and development specialists.[38]

5. No justice for rape victims in Afghanistan, 2013

A few weeks ago, a woman named Guldasta was raped by four armed men in Ghor Province of Afghanistan. While her rapists assaulted her, four of their friends were guarding the woman's house to prevent interventions. Days later, Guldasta's family fought back and took the case to local authorities; however, either unwilling or unable, the government failed them in providing justice.

Unfortunately, rape happens everywhere [in the world], but what is particular about Afghanistan, and a few other countries, is that the vast majority of Times, the raped, and not the rapist, is punished. This horrid phenomenon caught worldwide attention this week as authorities in UAE finally released a Norwegian woman who was arrested after reporting her sexual assault while on a business trip.

This happens in Afghanistan all the time. What's worse is that beyond the immediate physical and emotional trauma comes a lasting social stigmatization of rape victims.

In Afghanistan, when a woman is raped, rarely does a man agree to marry her because a woman is respected for her virginity, and regardless of how her hymen is broken, she must be punished. In addition to that, if a woman who is raped becomes pregnant, it is likely that she will have to marry the man who savagely disrespected her soul and body. That is, if she is lucky and not imprisoned by the government for "adultery" or has not committed suicide already. After getting married to her rapist, she must tolerate being raped- though according to Afghan law marital rape is not considered rape- every night until she dies or, sometimes self immolates. In addition to keeping her husband's bed warm, she must wash, clean, and cook for him, nourish his children, honor his family and guests, work on his barley fields, and even care for his livestock without any pay.

Guldasta will forever be called "dishonorable (badnaam)." All her friends and relatives will whisper with pity, "Poor thing. She has been dishonored." Guldasta, not her rapists, will carry the title with her until she dies. Her husband and father will also be called "dishonored." They will say, "Their honor has been raped," because she is considered their property and not an individual with her own honor and pride. Once she is raped, her family has lost honor, too.

As for the rapists, their honor will remain intact. No one thinks of controlling the bodies and minds of the rapists. They will be treated as if their loss of control is natural and part of their manhood and male instincts. Men get angry and rape, and they are not "dishonorable" and if they are imprisoned, chances are they will be released in a few months.

After being raped, Guldasta will become a lesson to others. When families want to prevent their daughters from going outside, they will say, "If you go out, you will become another Guldasta." People will stop their sons from standing up to warlords and rapists and warn, "Better remain silent or else your mother will have the same faith as Guldasta."

Guldasta's problem is not only the armed and powerful men who raped her and the government that failed to protect her rights; it is a society in which being raped is a bigger shame than raping. Rape will not vanish until we have combated the culture of rape, which treats women only worthy for their virginity or because they are the honor and property of the men in the family. Rape will not decrease unless we learn to respect women, especially after they are raped.

The culture of rape will not end unless we learn to shame and dishonor "badnaam" the rapists, not the women they have raped.[39]

6. Rape victims more stigmatized than the rapists, 2009

Rape victims in Afghanistan are more stigmatized than the rapists. Women who are raped can be and often are punished, while their male counterparts rarely face jail Time when accused of rape. Women are often punished as "fornicators" under adultery laws. Women are often persuaded to marry their rapist in hopes of restoring honor to her family. This is also done so the rapist can avoid facing charges. Thus putting women in the, very often dangerous, position of either marrying the man who raped and attacked them or facing honor crimes, possibly murder, at the hands of their own family members.[40]

7. Ten-year-old rape survivor faces "honour" killing , 2014

Help save a ten-year old girl from "Honor Killing"

[Amnesty International distributed this information as a bulletin, requesting readers to write various Afghan government officials to take action to save the girl.]

Brishna, a ten-year old girl from Kunduz province in Afghanistan was raped by a local mullah in May 2014. She is at risk of an "honour" killing by family and community members. The women's rights defender who assists her is facing death threats. Shortly after Brishna was raped on 1 May, she was admitted to a hospital for treatment with the assistance of the organisation Women for Afghan Women. During her stay in hospital, family and community members threatened to kill her.

The head of the Women for Afghan Women's shelter, Dr Hassina Sarwari, reported to a journalist that when she came to collect Brishna from the hospital to take her to the shelter, the girl's aunt told her that male relatives wanted to "kill her and dump her in the river." In July, after Brishna had spent two months in the shelter, local police took her from the shelter and returned her to her family despite the risk to her life. The local mullah accused of raping the girl has since been arrested and charged with rape of a minor. He has been transferred to a prison in Kabul and is awaiting trial.

Medical tests confirm that the girl is a pre-pubescent child and that she was subjected to a violent rape. Rape victims are at risk of "honour" killing as they are deemed to have brought "shame" on their family by an act of which they are the victims. Dr Sarwari has also received death threats from the girl's family, religious leaders, and powerful members of her community for her role in protecting Brishna. She continues to receive death threats, and she fears for her life.

Additional Information

In Afghanistan, women and girls are seen to be the embodiments of family honour. They are often the first to pay the price if perceived to have offended custom, tradition or so-called honour. Women who are assumed to have had sexual relations outside marriage (zina) are widely perceived to have brought "shame" on their families and are at risk of "honour" killing, either on the initiative of their male family members or the direction or local councils comprised of male elders.

Rape victims, too, are at risk of "honour" killing as they are deemed to have brought "shame" on their family by an act of which they are the victims. Discrimination against women and the proximity between the formal and informal justice systems is highlighted in the leniency and often lack of penal sanctions in cases of "honour" killings. Evoking honour as offences to custom and tradition is often an accepted defence in cases of killing of women and girls.

However, most cases of "honour" killings will not come before the formal judicial system, as families will tend to mete out punishments sanctioned by a community justice mechanism such as the shuras or jirgas (tribal councils). It is difficult to determine exactly how many women and girls in Afghanistan fall victims to "honour" killings. but, according to the Afghan Independent Human Rights Commission (AIHRC), between January 2011 and May 2013, two hundred and forty-three cases of "honour" killings were recorded.

Currently, "honour" killings are not criminalized under Afghanistan's Elimination of Violence Against Women (EVAW) law as a form of violence against women and women and girls. Rather, articles three hundred and ninety four to thirty hundred and ninety seven of the Penal Code address the crime of murder, but the offence is mitigated when it involves an "honour" killing, reducing the sentence to a term "not exceeding two years."[41]

8. Violence against women, 120 interviews, 2009

I summarize the following from a Human Rights Watch publication.

Violence against women [and girls] in Afghanistan is endemic....The forms of violence include rape, physical violence, forced marriage, and "honor killings." A "traditional" settlement for example, includes giving a female member of the perpetrator's family to the victim's family in marriage (a practice known as baad, where a woman is given as "compensation" or "retribution" for a crime). Most of the information in this Human Rights Watch report is based on more than one hundred twenty interviews Human Rights Watch conducted in 2009 in several Afghan provinces.

There are so many disputes between families and tribes, and too often they take personal revenge using the easiest victim— a child, a girl, a woman. Violence against women and girls in Afghanistan, including domestic violence, sexual harassment, and rape, is endemic. Too often, as soon as a girl starts menstruation, she is married. That can be as young as eleven or twelve. Physically and mentally she is not complete, it is dangerous for her. We meet girls who are thirteen years old with three children already, looking like thirty-year-old women. So many of the cases Human Rights Watch deals with have child marriage or marriage by force at the heart of them—cases of violence, running away, self-immolation and other suicide attempts.

Forced marriage and child marriage in Afghanistan remain widespread and socially accepted. Though the data on prevalence varies, all surveys indicate that well over half of all marriages are forced or involve girls under age sixteen. Forced marriage includes situations in which women and girls must marry without their consent, face threats or violence, are kidnapped, or are traded through informal dispute mechanisms. Sexual activity and pregnancy can be extremely dangerous and unhealthy for young girls, especially in Afghanistan where access to healthcare is extremely poor. Afghanistan has the second highest rate of maternal mortality in the world, with 1,700 women or girls dying per 100,000 live births.

A case study illustrates the danger of defying an arranged marriage. Fahima (not her real name) was forced by her family to marry. She was 22 years old at the time. She loved a certain boy, but her family forced to marry someone else. The family didn't ask her opinion. They called her names and threatened her. Fahima said, "I know they would have hurt me if I didn't agree." Though she had never met the man her family was forcing her to marry, eventually she felt she had no choice. She believed her parents were financially motivated to marry their choice and she thinks her parents married her three older sisters for money. One human rights observer said, "The family of the fiancé would get 300,000 Afghanis (or 6,000USD) for her, and that's why they didn't want to allow her to escape the engagement". In other words, a forced marriage in some cases can have a strong monetary incentive.

After seven months of engagement, Fahima still had not met the fiancé chosen by her family who remained in his home country of Iran. She ran away to Kabul with the man that she wanted to marry in order to marry. Under Afghan civil law, Fahima had the right to break off the engagement and marry someone else. But her brothers came to Kabul and took her to the police station. The police looked at her marriage certificate and heard her story. She said she'd committed no crime, but the police sent her and her husband to court. The court said she had two choices—go with her brothers or go to jail. She chose to go to jail because she knew that if she went with her brothers they would kill her.

It is important to note that there is no crime of "running away" in Afghan law or in Sharia law, despite the widespread actions of police and judges to the contrary. Women activists describe the use of this charge by law enforcement officials as driven primarily by the deep-seated customary view that young women and girls should not challenge cultural norms by asserting their independence and daring to voice complaints about their treatment in the home. In other words, cultural norms outweigh more modern and liberal law.

Fahima says, "I didn't do anything wrong, but I'm a woman so what can I do? My brothers are Pashtun, they've got a bad reputation, that's why I'm scared of them. They will definitely kill me when they have the chance." [The Taliban are primarily ethnic Pashtun. They held power in Afghanistan in part of the 1990's and became known for their barbaric brutality, tribal "traditions", and abusive treatment of women and girls. When they took over 2021 they were especially violent as I describe in Chapter 9.][42]

9. "Running away" from violence, 2012

I summarize the following from another Human Rights Watch publication.

Threats and attacks against women and girls in Afghanistan are common. "Honor killings" are a frequent occurrence in Afghanistan, and many women and girls interviewed for this report told Human Rights Watch they had been threatened with, or believed they were at risk of being killed by members of their families or in-laws. At times, even execution by stoning is practiced. Not surprisingly, the overwhelming majority of married women and girls interviewed for this report say that they did not marry by choice. Often they meet their husband on their wedding day and then immediately move to his household, where hostility and physical and emotional abuse from the husband, his other wives, or his family are common. "Running away" is not an offense found in the Afghan Penal Code. However, women and girls in Afghanistan have long faced punishment from family and local governing bodies for leaving home without permission.

The following is a case story about Tamina "running away." Tamina, seventeen, fell in love with a boy, whose name is Faisal. Tamina said the reason for her family's opposition to her marrying Faisal was that she already had been engaged to Sayed as a baby, and that Faisal was a "stranger" not related to their family. A week later Tamina and Faisal ran away. He picked her up from school and she fled with just the clothes she was wearing. They got married before a mullah the same day and then they hid in another city for three months. When they ran away, Faisal's family fled as well out of fear that

Tamina's father would take reprisal on them. At last Tamina's father and her brothers found them and took Faisal's father to jail. Tamina said that her grandmother told her, "Say that Faisal kidnapped you, otherwise your brothers will kill you." After some arguing Tamina and Faisal were both arrested for "running away." Tamina was sentenced to one year in jail for "running away," but Faisal was sentenced to ten years. Her brothers said, "Even if he is in jail ten years, when he is out of jail we will kill him and when you are out of jail, we will kill you."

At least twenty two of the fifty eight women and girls interviewed for this report said they believed they would face dangers following release. These dangers range from continued beatings and domestic abuse to homelessness to murder by a husband or family member. Many described specific threats and warnings they had received from family members who visited them in prison.

Again, this second Human Rights Watch report notes that, historically, some communities have sanctioned "honor" killings in which a woman could be killed by her own relatives for bringing "dishonor" upon the family by conduct perceived as breaching community norms of sexual behavior—including being a victims of sexual violence. And this is exactly the situation that Maryam, the central figure of this book, faced back in Chapter 1. Her family is not the exception to the rule but rather the rule of the culture of too many Afghans.[43]

10. Law on elimination of violence against women, 2013

The Afghan government's failure to respond effectively to violence against women undermines the already perilous state of women's rights. President Hamid Karzai's endorsement…of a statement by a national religious council calling women "secondary," prohibiting violence against women only for "un-Islamic" reasons, and calling for segregating women and girls in education, employment, and in public raises questions about the government's commitment to protecting women. The minister of justice's description of battered women shelters as sites of "immorality and prostitution" deepens that skepticism…

The Law on Elimination of Violence Against Women, adopted in 2009, remains largely unenforced. Women and girls who flee forced marriage or domestic violence are often treated as criminals rather than victims. As of spring 2012, four-hundred women and girls were in prison and juvenile detention for the "moral crimes" of running away from home or sex outside marriage.[44]

11. Execution by stoning, 2013

KABUL, Afghanistan — When …I read a draft law prepared by Afghan government officials that reintroduced execution by stoning [emphasis added] as the punishment for the "crime" of adultery, I was horrified but not that surprised.

Heather Barr is the senior Afghanistan researcher at Human Rights Watch.[45]

12. Survey of 1,051 women regarding violence, 2013

Violence is widespread

Violence against women is considered a widespread and undeniable reality in Afghanistan's society. The present report covers different types of violence against women in the first 6 months [of the Muslim year starting March 21, 2012]....Besides statistical information, the report also presents illustrative cases of violence that tell a horrendous reality [Page 1].

Violence against women in Afghanistan occurs in various forms... the most common types... are physical, sexual, economic, and verbal, and psychological.... According to our findings, one thousand and fifty one women suffered from different types of violence. These types of violence experienced by those women exceed three thousand three hundred and thirty one instances. The difference between actual cases (individuals) and statistical instances emanates from the fact that many women experienced two to three different types of violence.

There were a total of eight hundred and eighty-nine instances of physical violence, eight hundred and eight instances of verbal and psychological violence, seven-hundred and fifteen instances of economic violence, two hundred and fifty six instances of sexual violence, and six hundred and sixty-three instances that could not be classified in one of these groups were reported [page 13].

Physical violence

According to AIHRC's research, [the predominate type of] violence against women is physical violence. During the covered period, eight hundred and eighty-nine instances of physical violence have been recorded. Among many instances of physical violence, [page 13] kicking (four hundred and seven), slapping (hundred and twenty-nine), and beating with a wire (hundred and five) were the most common acts of physical violence. Moreover, pulling out hair (seventy-eight), using a knife (forty-one), and beating with a stick are further common instances of physical violence... Pushing (twenty-six), burning (twenty), using stones or soil (sixteen), using a weapon (eleven), beating with a gun butt (four), amputation (two), poisoning (two), spraying acid (two)... are other kinds of physical violence...

Sexual violence

Sexual violence is a common but socially and culturally hidden form of violence against women....talking about and enlarging upon sexual violence is taboo in Afghanistan's traditional society. However, an increase in reported cases was observed over the last few years. The recorded data by AIHRC shows that [out of three-thousand three hundred and thirty-one instances of violence] two hundred and fifty six instances of sexual violence...Sexual violence was experienced in many ways, such as forced sexual violence (seventy-one), demand for illegal sex/anal sex (sixty-two), and acts of sexual insult/humiliation (fifty). Forced prostitution (eighteen), extramarital affair (twenty-seven), forced abortion... and other ways...

Sexual violence, specifically in traditional societies like Afghanistan, has many social, cultural, and economic consequences. Raped women face new hardships, not just from the direct physical injuries but also from the psychological impact, which increases the risk of being infected by HIV/AIDS or having an unwanted pregnancy. The stigma attached to rape threatens women who speak out about the abuses to be abandoned by their husbands, ostracized by the community, left with no economic assets or income, and put her at risk of further human rights violations and deteriorated health. (Söderberg Jacobson, Agneta (2009) "Security on Whose Terms? If Men and Women Were Equal. Introduction," Kvinna till Kvinna Report, Women's Empowerment Projects: 6-16, p. 43.)

Verbal and psychological violence

A common type of violence that is rarely recognised as such is verbal and psychological violence. Insulting and threatening, however, can seriously affect women's personality and psychology and have drastic consequences in their personal and social life. Humiliating and degrading behaviours against women occur in all spheres of society, inside the family as well as in public spaces, and put women in a dangerous subject position. Observations show that continued verbal and psychological violence can result in self-immolation and other drastic outcomes. The eight hundred eight instances have been reported by the AIHRC staff during the covered period, including insulting and humiliating (two hundred and fifty nine), condemning women's personality or behaviour (hundred and eighty-five), threats to kill (hundred and fity-four), threats to divorce and taking the child (fifty-three), threats to abandon (forty-eight), insulting for not having a child (25), threats to expulse from home (twenty-three), threats to remarry or take another wife (twenty-one), playing a prank or mocking (seventeen), threats to rape her relatives… Due to the low recognition of the occurrence of verbal and psychological violence the actually expected number exceeds the statistical number by many Times and only a small number of cases become public.

Other instances of violence

Violence against women is not limited to the aforementioned boundaries, but there are other forms and types of violence imposed on women. A total of six-hundred and sixty-one instances have been registered during the period of investigation, including prevention from education (twenty-two)…prevention from visiting relatives (seven), lack of freedom to choose their spouse (seventy three), forced marriage (hundred and three), forced divorce (thirty-four), early marriage (sixty-five), taking high dowry (eighty-one), expulsion from home (hundred and eighty-seven) and others (fifty-three). Due to the widespread occurrence of these types of violence against women in the society, there is less social and cultural reaction against them. These types of violence are often considered ordinary or normal and are accepted as common practices. As the presented data shows, forced and early marriage, expulsion from home, or receiving high dowries occur frequently in Afghanistan and are rarely considered as violence against women. In reality, however, these practices have far-reaching negative impacts on women's life, personality, health and social and economic conditions. Early marriages, for example, have devastating physical and psychological impacts on young girls. Harmful traditional practices and customs are the main reasons for the continuation of these forms of violence. However, the category of "other instances" contains many kinds of violence that happened against women during… [The period of this survey], but along with many categories and instances, honor killing and rape is very alerting. During the covered period of the report, thirty-two instances of rape and more than sixty instances of honor killing have been collected and reported by AIHRC. This record is not classified into the five categories of violence.

Case story: Fifteen-year-old girl raped, beaten and lashed

A fifteen-year-old girl reports about her experience of being raped, beaten, and lashed in a quite [sic] secure and educated district in Ghazni province:

"One day in the month of Ramadan, I went to a tailor's shop where both the tailor and his assistant were present. After a while, the tailor asked his assistant to go out and bring something from the bazaar for him. When the assistant left the shop, the tailor took my hands and brought me to the closet. He asked me to have sex with him and I denied it and tried to shout, but his palm was faster. He put it in my mouth and forcedly raped me. He then threatened me not to disclose the case. Days later, around four pm, I went with my younger sister to our lands to collect some almonds, where suddenly a villager beat me with a long stick and took me to my paternal uncle's house. I saw around fifty men from my village gathered in the house. They beat me as well and asked me with whom I have had a relationship. After continued beating and under the pain I felt, I finally admitted that a tailor raped me.

"Thereafter, the district governor and other district officials heard about my case and put the perpetrator in a detention centre, but only for one night. Then, the villagers selected a representative and sent him to the district governor to ask not to put the case forward and to avoid an official process. They urged the governor to release the perpetrator and to send the case back to the villagers for resolving and taking the final decision. The decision-makers were elders and clergies who finally convinced the governor to release the perpetrator. Consequently, after the perpetrator was released, the clergies and elders decided to have a large meeting in order to make a decision and to finalise my case. Four days later, four clergy asked me to answer their questions, which lasted about fifteen minutes. I told them that the tailor raped me, but they did not accept my answer and said that my claim was not reliable. They finally decided to lash me a hundred times, while the perpetrator was released because of his denying. I rejected their decision and said that I would appeal for an official due process. But they did not let me go. Hours later, they took me to "Bidak" desert in order to lash me. Many men and women were watching the scene from their roofs and the peaks of the surrounding hills. They forced me to rest on the ground, then one of the famous commanders [was] ordered to lash me hundred times, but he lashed me one more ([making it] hundred and one)."

Perpetrators and places of violence

The findings and information collected by regional and provincial offices of the AIHCR clearly show that acts of violence take almost exclusively place within the victim's own family, making ninety percent of all reported cases. Against general opinion, the findings of this report show that those family members who are the closest to the victims are the main perpetrators of violence. On the long list with perpetrators, the victims' husbands take the first place with two thousand three hundred and twenty-nine [or seventy percent, two thousand three hundred and twenty–nine perpetrators out of three-thousand three hundred and thirty one] reported cases, followed by father (hundred and eighty-two), parent (hundred and fifty two), fiancé (hundred and fourteen), brother (ninety-eight), brother-in-law (ninety-two), mother (forty-nine), sister-in-law (husband's sister) (thirty-five), victims sons (thirty-one), paternal uncle (twenty-three), maternal uncle (seventeen), sister (twelve), teacher (eight) and others. In other words, the victims' husbands commit seventy percent of all violent acts. This appalling figure reveals a bitter reality of domestic violence that often remains in the dark of family structures.

[All of the male perpetrators equal out of three thousand three hundred and thirty one instances of violence or eighty-seven percent. The violence and abuse that Maryam and Sarya endured was by far at the hands of her mother or directed by the "bad" aunt, followed by what her father and one older brother committed. This is counter to the preponderance of perpetrators being male family members in the survey cited above. Her mother and the bad aunt had their own motives explained in other chapters; however, they were acting within a context where violence against women and girls was rampant, and I think made it more permissible for a female to exact the violence. As I describe in the chapter about Maryam's girlfriends, once in Canada, Maryam didn't have to look far to find Afghan-Canadian girlfriends to be violent against her.]

Consequences of violence

The figures for mental or psychological damage are distressing, portraying that mental disability [emotional duress] is with thousand and thirty-one reported instances at a considerable distance from other serious consequences. In sixty-one cases perpetrated violence led to physical disabilities, cases provoked injuries, and four limbs fractures were reported. In a total of fifteen cases, death [homicide] was the result of violence. Thirty-five victims committed self-immolation, and in a total of seventy incidences women attempted suicide. These numbers are appalling and reveal the darkest consequences of violence against women. In addition to physical and psychological harms, violence against women inflects irreparable damages on the social and economic situation of women in the society. Demand for divorce (five hundred and ninety seven), divorce (two hundred and ninety nine), escaping from home (three hundred and fifty six)… are other observed outcomes.

[I must comment on the thirty-five cases of death by self-immolation and seventy instances of attempted suicide. These numbers are low compared to the total number of three thousand three hundred and thirty one cases of violence on thousand and fifty-one women. As pointed out below under constraints, "the actual number of victims is… expected to be much higher." When Maryam told us of actual completed or attempted acts of self-immolation (one by a sister-in-law over humiliation and trauma stemming from a rape by the Taliban), I was very shocked. It was so far beyond my realm of experience. In my knowledge of Canada, the United States or European countries, I am not aware of self-immolation at all.

I think if that happened it would be intensely covered by the media because it is simply unheard of. The seventy instances of attempted suicide is alarming also.]

Constraints of collecting data

Although efforts by the Commission were unremitting, many obstacles were faced. Truly, a main problem in gathering the data was the lack of security that resulted in the inaccessibility of certain areas. Additionally, embedded traditionalism and widespread customs in many parts of Afghanistan do not allow women to talk freely about violence they have endured. Such practices prevent an accurate study as women are considered as a property or object of men and intervention into private space is not allowed. As a result AIHRC members were not able to pose questions directly to the affected people, and the collection of cases was only partially feasible. Moreover, armed groups such as the Taliban hampered AIHRC activities, and it was sometimes impossible to collect data and conduct interviews. A further obstacle consisted in the limitation of Time and transport facilities, which made it difficult to visit remote places on a regular basis....the above-mentioned obstacles made all-encompassing research impossible, and the actual number of victims is, therefore, expected to be much higher.[46]

13. A 15-year-old girl is locked in the basement, 2013

In December 2011, police rescued a fifteen-year-old girl in Baghlan Province after they found her locked in a basement bathroom, having had her fingernails pulled out and being forced into prostitution by her thirty-year-old husband and in-laws… [After extensive legal proceedings] the Kabul Appellate Court ordered that all three defendants be released from prison.[47]

14. Self-immolation, 2013

"Killing women in Afghanistan is an easy thing. There's no punishment," Suraya Pakzad, who runs women's shelters in several provinces, told Reuters in her office in the western city of Herat. She cited recent cases in which women had been publicly stoned [emphasis added] as Afghan troops looked on. "Laws are improved, but implementation of those laws are in the hands of warlords... I think we are going backwards."

Another sign that rights for women have been rolled back in recent years is a rise in cases of self-immolation, a desperate last resort for women in abusive situations. The burn unit of Herat hospital, one of two in Afghanistan, admitted a record number of women who had attempted to set themselves on fire in 2012. [emphasis added] The head of the ward said he was reluctant to speak out because of threats from relatives. "If they come with a high percentage of body surface burns... we cannot save them," Dr Ghafar Bawar told Reuters during a recent visit to his ward. "After disfigurement, they have a very hard life." Bawar also treated patients who had suffered burns in attacks. He agreed there was a culture of impunity and that some assaults were not reported to officials for fear of reprisal.

[Self-immolation is self-violence as opposed to violence perpetrated on a victim. However, I think it reflects a normalization of violence, making the plight of women and girls so distressing that they find self-harm and destruction as a way out. Another way of saying it is that self-destruction is a more certain way of violence than running away.]

For instance, a neighbor had brought in a woman and her four-year-old child the night before. The father had thrown a burning blanket over them as they slept, setting them alight. Both died of their injuries, but the neighbor was too afraid to report the case to the authorities.[48]

15. Taliban gang rapes two midwives

According to local activists, Taliban fighters also raped female relatives and killed family members, including children, of police commanders and soldiers, especially those working for Afghan Local Police (ALP). The Taliban also burnt down the families' houses and looted their belongings. The relative of a woman who worked as a midwife in Kunduz maternity hospital told Amnesty International how Taliban fighters gang-raped and then killed her and another midwife because they accused them of providing reproductive health services to women in the city.[49]

16. Lack of investigation of gender-based violence, 2021

[The U.S. State Department annually evaluates human rights for countries around the world, including those regarding the rights of women. For the year 2021, it evaluated those rights both before and after the takeover of the country by the Taliban on August 15th.]

The human rights issues included credible reports of…lack of investigation of and accountability for gender-based violence, including but not limited to cases of violence against women, including domestic… partner violence, sexual violence, child, early and forced marriage, and other harmful practices; trafficking in persons for forced labor and commercial sexual exploitation…[50]

17. Restrictions on women and girls increase under the Taliban, 2022

The despair created by the loss of gains women and girls had made in Afghanistan before 2021 is devastating. Over the past fifteen months [since the Taliban takeover in August 2021], Afghan women and girls have been facing increased restrictions that have limited their access to education, their ability to seek employment, their freedom of movement, and their freedom to exercise so many other rights.[51]

18. "We are erased", 2022

"We are erased," said Mahbooba Seraj, a human rights activist from Afghanistan. "Today human rights in Afghanistan do not exist. Women of Afghanistan do not exist for the Taliban." She chose to stay in the country after the Taliban takeover [in August 2021] to be a witness of what was going to be happening and be able to tell the world about it, she said. Seraj was one of the speakers during a discussion on the plight of women and girls in Afghanistan during the [UN] Human Rights Council.

Since the Taliban took power in August 2021, the human rights situation of women and girls in Afghanistan has deteriorated. The Taliban have "deprived women and girls of their human rights, removed women from spheres of public life, and undone women's agency," said Ilze Brands Kehris, Assistant Secretary-General for Human Rights.

"Women have nowhere to go to seek justice and redress in today's Afghanistan," she said. Nowhere else in the world has there been as widespread and all-encompassing a rollback, stated Richard Bennet, Special Rapporteur on Afghanistan. "Edicts have been imposed that not only restrict women and girls' daily lives; they rob them of their futures and strip them of their identity and dignity," said Bennet.

In his report, Bennet states that within the last thirteen months, there has been a "staggering regression in women and girls' enjoyment of civil, political, economic, social and cultural rights." Several edicts and decrees have been put into effect that have limited women's and girls' rights, including suspension of secondary education for girls, enforcing mandatory hijab wearing in public, and banning women from traveling without being accompanied by a close male family member (mahram).

"Women belonging to ethnic, religious, or linguistic minority groups, as well as women with disabilities, and women without male family members have been suffering from intersectional discrimination," Brands Kehris said. The increasing constraints on women's freedom of movement have significantly affected their ability to access health care and education, earn a living, seek protection, and escape situations of violence, the report states.

Moreover, the Taliban have dissolved human rights oversight mechanisms, such as the Afghan independent Human Rights Commission, and dismantled specialized courts for gender-based violence and victims' support services, Brands Kehris added. "Their subjective and extremist interpretation of Islam is antithetical to the international human rights law, their draconian misogynistic form of rule does not reflect our religion, our culture, and our values."[52]

19. Gender inequality

The Afghanistan Gender Inequality Index Rank is 157. The Gender Inequality Index is a composite measure reflecting inequality between women and men in three different dimensions: reproductive health (maternal mortality ratio and adolescent birth rate), empowerment (share of parliamentary seats held by women and share of the population with at least some secondary education), and labour market participation (labour force participation rate). The ranking is out of hundred ninety three UN Member states.[53]

20. Gap ranks

The Afghanistan Global Gender Gap Index Rank is 156. The Global Gender Gap Index benchmarks national gender gaps on economic, political, education, and health criteria. The ranking is out of 193 UN Member states.[54]

21. Taliban bars aid groups from hiring women

For an idled worker at a Kabul-based aid group, Abaad, that helps abused Afghan women, frightened and often tearful calls are coming in not only from her clients but also from her female colleagues.

A Dec. 24 [2022] order from the Taliban barring aid groups from employing women is paralyzing deliveries that help keep millions of Afghans alive and threatening humanitarian services country-wide. The United Nations estimates that 85% of nongovernmental aid organizations in Afghanistan have partially or fully shut down operations because of the ban, which is the Taliban's latest step to drive women from public life.

Abaad was among those suspending its work. Its female employees provided support and counseling to women who endured rape, beatings, forced marriages, or other domestic abuse. Female clients told an Abaad worker that without the group's help, they fear they will wind up on Kabul's streets. For the worker herself and for thousands like her across Afghanistan, they depend on their paychecks to survive in a broken economy where aid officials say 97% of the population is now in poverty or at risk of it. One colleague told her she was contemplating suicide.[55]

22. Adverse childhood experience

Maryam's experience with abuse and violence and that experience of women and girls in Afghanistan documented elsewhere in this Appendix is put into perspective by a study with a large sample size in America. It's safe to say, based on other sources in this Appendix, the incidence of adverse childhood experiences is substantially greater in Afghanistan than in America. A study of over seventeen thousand adults in America concluded that One in eight people responded positively to the questions: "As a child, did you witness your mother sometimes, often, or very often pushed, grabbed, slopped, or had something thrown at her?" "As a child, did you witness your mother sometimes, often, or very often kicked, bitten, hit with a fist, or hit with something hard?"

…People typically don't grow up in a household where one brother is in prison, but everything else is fine. They don't live in families where their mother is regularly beaten, but life is otherwise funky-dory. Incidents of abuse are never stand-alone events. And for each additional adverse experience reported, the toll in later damages increases.[56]

23. UN and AP: Afghanistan is world's most repressive country for women, 2023

ISLAMABAD (AP) — Since the Taliban takeover of Afghanistan in August 2021, the country has become the most repressive in the world for women and girls, deprived of virtually all their basic rights, the United Nations said in grim assessments on International Women's Day. The U.N. Mission said in a statement Wednesday that Afghanistan's new rulers have shown an almost "singular focus on imposing rules that leave most women and girls effectively trapped in their homes."

Despite initial promises of a more moderate stance, the Taliban have imposed harsh measures since seizing power as U.S. and NATO forces were in the final weeks of their pullout from Afghanistan after two decades of war.

Girls are banned from education beyond sixth grade and women are barred from working, studying, traveling without a male companion, and even going to parks or bath houses. Women must also cover themselves from head to toe and are barred from working at national and international non-governmental organizations, disrupting the delivery of humanitarian aid. "Afghanistan under the Taliban remains the most repressive country in the world regarding women's rights," Roza Otunbayeva, special representative of the U.N. secretary-general and head of the U.N. political mission in Afghanistan, said in a statement.

She later told the U.N. Security Council in New York that "the Taliban claim to have united the country, but they have also severely divided it by gender." The Taliban tell the U.N. "that this gender segregation is not a significant issue and is being addressed" and "they say they should be judged on other achievements," she said. At a time when Afghanistan needs to recover from decades of war, Otunbayeva said, "half of the country's potential doctors, scientists, journalists, and politicians are shut away in their homes, their dreams crushed and their talents confiscated."

"It has been distressing to witness their methodical, deliberate, and systematic efforts to push Afghan women and girls out of the public sphere," she added. The restrictions, especially the bans on education and NGO work, have drawn fierce international condemnation. But the Taliban have shown no signs of backing down, claiming the bans are temporary suspensions in place allegedly because women were not wearing the Islamic headscarf, or hijab, correctly and because gender segregation rules were not being followed.

As for the ban on university education, the Taliban government has said that some of the subjects being taught were not in line with Afghan and Islamic values. "Confining half of the country's population to their homes in one of the world's largest humanitarian and economic crises is a colossal act of national self-harm," Otunbayeva said.

"It will condemn not only women and girls, but all Afghans, to poverty and aid-dependency for generations to come," she warned. "It will further isolate Afghanistan from its own citizens and from the rest of the world." At a carpet factory in Kabul, women who were former government employees or high school and university students now spend their days weaving carpets.

"We all live like prisoners, we feel that we are caught in a cage," said Hafiza, 22, who goes only by her first name and who used to be a first-year law student before the Taliban banned women from attending classes at her university. "The worst situation is when your dreams are shattered, and you are punished for being a woman."

Another worker at the factory, 18-years-old Shahida, who also uses only one name, said she was in 10th grade at one of Kabul high schools when her education was cut short. "We just demand from the (Taliban) government to reopen schools and educational centers for us and give us our rights," she said.

An Afghan women's rights campaigner, Zubaida Akbar, told the Security Council that since the Taliban seized power "the rights of Afghan women and girls have been decimated through over 40 decrees." "The Taliban have sought not only to erase women from public life, but to extinguish our basic humanity," said Zubaida, who spoke on behalf of the rights group Freedom Now that deals with 20 mostly women-led grassroots movements inside Afghanistan. "There is one term that appropriately describes the situation of Afghan woman today — gender apartheid."

Alison Davidian, the special representative for UN Women in Afghanistan, said: "The implications of the harm the Taliban are inflicting on their own citizens goes beyond women and girls." No officials from the Taliban-led government were available for comment.

At the Security Council, the U.N.'s Otunbayeva said there is a faction in the Taliban that doesn't agree with the crackdown on women and girls and understands that attention must be paid to the real needs of all Afghans.

"Perhaps it can eventually execute a change of direction," she said. "But time is running short. Global crises are multiplying. Demands on donor resources are multiplying as the availability of those resources diminishes." Ahead of Wednesday's observances of International Women's Day, about 200 Afghan female small business owners put together an exhibition of their products in Kabul. Most complained of losing business since the Taliban takeover. "I don't expect Taliban to respect women's rights," said one of them, Tamkin Rahimi. "Women here cannot practice (their) rights and celebrate Women's Day, because we cannot go to school, university or go to work, so I think we don't have any day to celebrate."

Ten of the 15 Security Council members issued a joint statement demanding that the Taliban immediately reverse all its oppressive measures against women and girls. "Recovery in Afghanistan cannot happen without women's full, equal and meaningful participation in all aspects of political, economic and social life," said the statement by Albania, Brazil, Ecuador,

France, Gabon, Japan, Malta, Switzerland, United Aarab Emirates and United Kingdom.[57]

24. Report: Mental health crisis worsens for Afghan women, 2023.

The mental health of Afghan women, who have suffered under harsh measures imposed by the Taliban since taking power two years ago, according to a joint report from three U.N. agencies…

Nearly seventy percent reported that feelings of anxiety, isolation, and depression had grown significantly worse between April and June, an increase from 57% in the preceding quarter, according to the report…

The women spoke of suffering from psychological problems, including depression, insomnia, loss of hope and motivation, anxiety, fear, aggression, isolation, increasingly isolationist behavior, and thoughts of suicide.[58]

Appendix 2 Implosion of a country

Demographics

Afghanistan had a population of about 40 million in the country in 2021.[59] Globally, an estimated 5.1 million Afghans lived outside their home country as of 2019.[60]

Globally, the diaspora as a percent of the home country population is interesting, as shown in Table 1. The size of the Afghan diaspora is 10[th,] but it is tied for second and third with Ukraine as a percent of its population. The Ukrainian outmigration has exploded since Russia invaded it in February 2022, making that explainable. Syria is number one in percent diaspora at 46% because of its over 10 years of civil war. Each of the countries with the top ten diaspora populations has their own history as to when the out- migrations occurred.

Table 1. Top 10 countries with the largest diaspora population in the world (in millions).

Country	Diaspora [61]	Population [62]	Diaspora (in %)
2019	2023		
1. India	17.5	1,380	1%
2. Mexico	11.8	129	9%
3. China	10.7	1,439	1%
4. Russia	10.5	146	7%
5. Syria	8.2	18	46%
6. Bangladesh	7.8	165	5%
7. Pakistan	6.3	221	3%
8. Ukraine	5.9	44	13%
9. Philippines	5.4	110	5%
10. Afghanistan	5.1	39	13%

*All figures are rounded.

Maryam's family members, cousins, and friends are spread far and wide, not just Canada. Maryam mentions the following countries the most in referring to them: Canada, Germany, and the UK (mostly London) followed by Turkey (often a steppingstone to Germany or the UK), the Ukraine (probably not since Putin started the war there), India, Canada, Norway, and a few others. However, according to Wikipedia, the numbers are different, as shown in Table 2. It's interesting how the countries where Maryam's family and friends live compared to the actual numbers in Table 2.

Table 2. Afghan population by country with Afghan Diaspora.

Country	Afghan diaspora population [63]
Iran	c. 3 million
Pakistan	1.2 million
Germany	337,000
US	300,000
United Arab Emirates	300,000
Russia	150,000
Turkey	130,000
Canada	125,000
UK	79,000
Sweden	61,000
Australia	52,000

*Years for these numbers are between 2020 and 2023. The source lists 25 other countries, from 52,000 to 300.

Two factors have driven Afghans from their homeland: a poor economy and prolonged war. In the 1970's, Afghanistan was beset with internal war and conflict. In the 1980's, the Soviet occupied devastated the country. The U.S. was against Soviet military occupation, so the U.S. armed the mujahadeen to oppose the Soviets and the Soviets finally gave up in the late 1980's. Commentators called this the Soviet's Viet Nam, the war that couldn't be won because the enemy, the native Afghans didn't fight a conventional war. They would strike and skirmish in the lowlands and then run and hide in the largely mountainous country. See map in Figure 19. Pakistan trained ethnic Pashtun in the early 1990's across the border in Pakistan, and they took on the name "Taliban." The Taliban took over Afghanistan for most of the 1990's and made it the only country in the world to prohibit girls and women from receiving an education. They also enforced strict dress codes for girls and women, and horrified Afghanistan and the world with draconian law enforcement, including beheading of prisoners in public stadiums. They were in control up to 9/11 in the year 2001. Immediately after 9/11, the U.S. chased Osama Bin Laden into Afghanistan because it determined he was the mastermind of the attack on the World Trade Center and the Pentagon.

Many thousands of U.S. troops descended on this country. As the years passed, the role of the U.S. morphed into getting rid of the Taliban. To do so, Obama changed its military strategy to train and advise the Afghan military. At its peak, the troop count of the U.S. and its allies rose to over 100,000. The Taliban's offense was to drop bombs on hospitals, girls' schools, mosques, public squares, and the like. It was easy for them to carry out this kind of warfare with low cost and low effort. It was hard for our troops and those of the allied nations to retaliate or gain ground on them. They would hide and be elusive in mountainous terrain or mix in with the civilian population. The U.S. and its allies used drones targeted at Taliban leaders, which were effective, but sometimes we would kill innocent civilians, which would send ripples of fear for the survivors.

Shabana was in a hospital in Kabul, and the Taliban dropped a bomb and killed several doctors and nurses and wounded many others. She was so close that she was injured by shrapnel. She was, of course, the most traumatized, but it rippled to the family, 20 or 50 members, depending on how you count it. Because of the tight and extensive family structures, many family members feel the pain of one of the family. It was a state of war. Maryam's family was fearful of visiting or moving to Kabul because these bombings tended to happen more in Kabul.

President Trump negotiated the withdrawal of the U.S. military with the Taliban in 2019 and 2020. Withdrawal was scheduled to be by September 11, 2021—symbolically twenty years after 9/11. President Biden came into office in January 2021, followed through on that plan, and pulled out the last 5,000 U.S. troops by mid-August. The quintessential picture was of this huge aircraft taxiing down the runway with desperate Afghans hanging on cowling around the wheels. It was very bad optics for Biden. Critics said Biden was disorganized and he was doing a terrible job of evacuating Canadians and Afghans. But then Biden oversaw the evacuation of over 100,000 people in less than four weeks, a mixture of both Canadians, Afghans who worked for the U.S. military, and their families.

In the lead up to that August, the Taliban quickly, in a matter of months, took over first rural areas, towns, smaller cities, and then provincial capitals such as Kunduz. By mid-August they had taken over all but a few small pockets of Afghanistan. Over the 20 years of the U.S. occupation, the U.S. and Western allies trained about 250,000 Afghans in methods of modern warfare and provided arms and equipment. That's how many Afghan national troops there were when we departed in August 2021. With the takeover by the Taliban the 250,000 Afghan national troops vanished, just evaporated instantly; why, it is not entirely clear. Also on arrival of the

Taliban in Kabul the President of Afghanistan disappeared. The Taliban took free reign and raped, pillaged, and committed all manner of atrocities on seemingly everyone who was not Taliban. This would render the country's implosion for the foreseeable future.

War implodes the country

This constant warfare drove out the more educated. This is often called the "brain drain," much as has happened with other war-torn countries. However, it is more than just a brain drain. Those educated people are the elements of a civilized society. The elements of the educated segment of Afghan society include reliable courts, the rule of law, fair enforcement of law, respect for fellow human beings, a working economy not dependent on money from non-governmental organizations or foreign governments, a strong middle class, moral, societal norms, and therefore functional families. Education was at all levels for boys and girls, men and women, medicine, business, IT, journalism, and on and on in the 1960's. In that time, more women than men were educated at universities, pictures show men and women wearing western clothes (particularly no hijabs or burkas for women).

With the Taliban taking control of the country in 2021, you can multiply the depravity by many fold. The allied military occupation provided some stability to the country, and NGO's provided extensive social support systems, both financial and programmatic. The Taliban kicked out nearly all of the NGO's. Even within the Taliban there are relatively moderate elements who tend to be more urban and educated. Then there are the more conservative, who tend to be more rural and less educated. Fifty years of war from 1970 to 2021 ravaged the country.

In short, as the educated people have left, the strong elements of a civil society have left with them, which has imploded the civilization leaving it uncivilized and to a great degree, tribal and barbaric. My theory is based on books, news from National Public Radio and BBC, and other media. It is also based on stories by Afghans themselves and stories from Afghan-Canadians.

Stories of implosion from the diaspora

I would get to meet many of Afghans who had been in Canada for 10 to 20 years or more. They all told me the same story. Afghanistan was the jewel of civilization on the Indian Sub-continent before 1970, as one Indian from the Asian subcontinent told me one time, in exasperation, about wars that ravaged Afghanistan from the 1970's onward to 2021.

I met many Afghans who told me of all the Afghans who moved to other countries, the diaspora. Even before Maryam moved in with us, the first time we were in public, we went down to a public square with upscale stores and fountains. It was very pleasant. There were not that many people around, but there was what appeared to be a family group, a few young kids, a woman in her 30's, another lady in her 50's, and an elderly woman dressed in clothes I would say were from the old country. Maryam looked over at them and said, "Those people are Afghan." Being the outgoing person she is, she walked over and started talking in her native Farsi—it was like this magnet, an inexorable force pulling her over to them. And sure enough, they were Afghan. It turns out that they all spoke Farsi, including the young kids. The old woman's eyes lit up, her words flowed like a fountain speaking to Maryam. She held Maryam's hand in both of her hands, holding onto Maryam like she was a treasure. From what I could decipher, the grandmother had not been out of Afghanistan long, and she missed Afghanistan and here was a little Afghan flower or a gem not long out of the homeland and she could hold onto to this treasure. I read into this that she was probably from a village in rural Afghanistan. I asked a guy in the group, "Yes, she is from a small village." I nearly fell over watching Maryam making this connection. I had lived in Toronto for over six years at that point, and I knew there were a lot of Muslims because of all of the women who wore hijabs. But I didn't realize how many Afghans there were in the area. I would come to find out how many.

It was the fifty-year-old woman who was the first to explain to me the effects of the decades-long war that has imploded the Afghan society and culture. Over ensuing years, I ran into many other Afghans through Maryam, and if it hadn't been for Maryam, I would not have gotten connected with these people. She was my introduction to a broader Afghan world. These Afghans felt comfortable with me asking probing questions about how their lives fit into the bigger picture of the Afghan diaspora and the conditions back in Afghanistan. In many cases, they were eagerly engaged in revealing their life story, as if telling their story not just to me but for the world to hear. To a person, every one of them verified the narrative of the implosion of the Afghan civilization brought on by the decades of war.

Here's another story from the diaspora. There was this Afghan-Canadian guy who worked as an officer in a bank whom I got to know. This time, I got to know this without Maryam being the link. In the course of the first conversation, it just came out that he was Afghan, so I told him about Maryam, and the conversation went from there. Over many visits, I got to learn about his background and how it fit in the bigger picture. He had moved with his family to Moscow when he was in high school. His father had been on the side of the Soviets in the 1980's, and the Soviets enabled these Afghan cooperators to move to Russia after they withdrew. Now the strange part was that some years later, he was able to come to Canada. I was never clear about what kind of visa he used. Nevertheless, he did make it to Canada. He said there were many who went on this route through Moscow to Canada. For me, that was strange, I had never heard of it before. Later, I did hear of Afghans who spent as many as twenty years while their children grew up in Russia, and then they came to Canada. He spoke nearly fluent English with a mild Farsi accent. He was in his 30's, and he happily returned to Afghanistan to arrange for his fiancé to come to Canada. There was pride in his voice—by returning to pick up his wife, he was bringing back his culture, a culture where he could have children and perpetuate the Afghan culture, in an Afghan-Canadian way. Notwithstanding this positive aspect, he, too, exactly verified the implosion idea. By the same token, taking his wife out of Afghanistan, extracting her in a sense, he was relieving her of living in the painful implosion going on back home.

Once I heard many consistent stories from the Afghan diaspora about the implosion of civil society in Afghanistan, I was able to determine that all the horrific stuff going in Maryam's family and community was, in fact, a reflection of larger segments of the Afghan society. I have been able to connect more dots to get a better picture. From what I can tell, there is a strong layer that is dysfunctional. Strong elements are barbaric and tribal. Too often life is cheap. It is full of family vendettas with horrific or even fatal consequences. Beneath contemporary 1970 to 2021, where war predominated, is the strong undertow of ancient barbarism and tribalism. In contrast to this, I should point out that there are many compassionate individuals who take care of others in need about whom Maryam has told us, namely Sayeed and Ismail.

Maryam, Jennifer, and I were talking and reflecting one day. I asked Maryam, "What will your life be like in 20 years?" She responds quickly, "I want to be educated!" Next question, "What will Afghanistan be like in 20 years?" Maryam and I agree, "The Taliban, conflict, degradation of women, poor education, poverty, etc."

Appendix 3 Hijabs, burqas, and the Taliban

Many Muslim women wear a hijab. Not all Muslim women wear a hijab, but you will know it when they do. It depends on the country and often personal preference. A hijab is a head scarf which is worn in a wide variety of ways. It can be covering her whole shoulders and everything on the face from the nose down, showing just the eyes in the more conservative fashion or in the more liberal fashion, showing her whole face and the hair nearest the forehead. Colors and patterns vary widely also. It can be from black to white and dull colors to bright, vivid colors. It can be no pattern, just one color, or intricate patterns. The most conservative fashion is to wear the hijab with a tunic worn to the ground.

Then there is the burqa or a burka, which is an enveloping outer garment that fully covers the body and the face. The eyes are covered with a mesh, which obscures the eyes. I have lived and travelled to many parts of the world, however, the first time I saw a burqa, I was shocked. This was at the Toronto Airport and, even as big as the airport is, chocked full of diversity, when I saw this woman in a burqa I was so shocked, I literally gasped. Momentarily, I was even a bit scared. This burqa just grabbed my eyes. I had seen movies of Muslim countries with women with hijabs and burkas, but this live burqa jumped out at me.

The most comparable garb I can think of is the Catholic nun in the black and white habit, which I would classify as coming from a bygone era, ancient even. The habit shields sexuality, and a burka makes sexuality invisible. As I understand it, the Taliban professes an ancient, if not distorted, interpretation of the Quran and associated cultural expressions. They call for the burqa over the liberal forms of the hijab. The Taliban has a spectrum of interpretations of the Quran, the hyper-conservative side which prevailed during their rule in the 1990's into 2001 when Western forces took over. Starting with their takeover in 2021 there has been a sort of tug-of-war between the two sides with the conservative side tending to prevail over the liberal.

An extract from an article written three weeks after the Taliban takeover in August 2021 follows.

"It has been three weeks since the Taliban announced a new order, prescribing a strict dress code for women, that they should not leave the house without real need and if they do, should wear what is termed 'sharia hijab', with face covered entirely, or except for the eyes. The order made a woman's 'guardian' – her father, husband, or brother – legally responsible for policing her clothing, with the threat to punish him if she goes outside bare-faced. We hear from women about how they and their families have responded to the order and to what extent the new rules or guidelines have been enforced. Dress codes may seem less consequential than other changes, such as sending women workers home from government offices, hindering women's travel, or stopping older girls from going to school. Still, instructing women to cover their faces in public seems symbolic of the Emirate's apparent desire to turn Afghan women into entirely invisible, private citizens again…"

Figure 2. Burqas.[64]

"What women wear outside the home varies across Afghanistan – from the burqa, known in Afghanistan as a *chadori*… to big, baggy dresses with pleated trousers, to tight jeans and long shirts or coats. It has been extremely rare for Afghan woman, even in recent years, to choose to be seen in public bare-headed, but the style of a headscarf can vary from a very long, full, Iranian-style scarf that covers the head and clothes (often called *chador namaz*, as many women also wear it to pray) to much shorter and colourful scarves. Scarves can be worn to cover or almost cover the hair, or be tied to leave just the eyes exposed *(niqab)*. The black scarves typically worn with an abaya often come with integral niqab and full face veil options, which can be changed depending on how 'exposed' a woman wants to be – she may feel differently about revealing her face at work, for example, or in the bazaar, or in a shared taxi or bus, or in her own neighbourhood. In Herat, some women wear a *magna,* which is made-to-fit and pulls on over the head. It may show some or no hair, and may cover the chin, but not the rest of the face."

"What women wear tends to differ with age, how conservative she, her family or her neighbours are, whether she works in paid employment and how safe or exposed she feels, and of course personal style. As a general rule, in Times and places where women and girls feel safer, where they are in greater numbers outside and in the workplace, and where probably also, their income is higher, clothing has tended to be more varied and more colourful, with some individuals wearing tighter-fitting clothing and smaller scarves, and more women showing their faces in public.

"The Taleban's new order [since their takeover in August 2021] has boiled all this variation down to two versions of what the Taleban consider to be 'sharia hijab' – either a burqa or "customary black clothing and shawl," that is not too thin or too tight, which is presumed to be a reference to the abaya and which should be worn with a niqab. In doing this, the Taleban have taken to the state the right to make decisions about people's personal lives which, in Afghanistan, would normally be the preserve of the family... [The order states that the burqa has been] 'part of Afghanistan's dignified culture for centuries.'"[65]

Figure 3. Hijabs worn by art students in Afghanistan before the Taliban rule.[66]

Figure 4. Burqas in Afghanistan, bright color prior to Taliban rule.[67]

Figure 5. Street Market in Afghanistan, women with burqas.[68]

Related to Taliban edicts about the hijab and burqa, early on after the Taliban takeover in 2021, the Taliban leadership said they would allow teenage girls to go to school. After some months, it came out that they would not let them go to school past the sixth grade, at the behest of the more conservative side, indicating a tug-of-war between the conservative and the liberal sides of the Taliban with the conservatives prevailing, much like in neighboring Iran.

Toronto has a very diverse population, including Muslims. In Toronto, there was a mosque less than one half a mile from our house. On Friday evenings, we would see large numbers of Muslims walking to the mosque because Friday is equivalent of the Sunday sabbath for Christians. A neighbor down the street who was the first person I had ever met from Bangladesh. What a wonderful man he was, so kind, in fact, so interested in the good of our neighborhood of 200 some houses, he was sort of a *de facto* mayor, always helping people. So I asked, "Shahin, how many nations are represented at the mosque." He thought a bit, and replied in decent enough English but with a Bangladeshi accent, "Well, Eric, I think maybe 100 countries." I thought, wow, there are about 200 countries in the world, and half of them are represented at this one mosque! Qualifying this is that another neighbor, Rashid (he wouldn't give his last name because he said it was too difficult to pronounce), and his wife were from South Africa with family roots in what is now Pakistan. He and his wife went to that mosque, and he said they were the only Muslims from South Africa. So that accounts for one of the 100 countries.

As we drove through our neighborhood and any neighborhood for many miles around, we would see women working, recreating, walking, and any other outdoor activity, many had hijabs on. Jennifer's mom was living with us at the time. Jennifer's dad was in the Navy for the first 20 years of their marriage, so she had lived in many places and was immersed in many different cultures. But she also grew up in the rather mono-cultural society of the rural Midwest. So Jennifer's mom and I were driving back into our neighborhood, and this 30-something Muslim woman was outside wearing her hijab and Levis, and mowing the grass. Jennifer's mom exclaims, "That's it! They either go all the way one way or another! If they wear a hijab they can't mow the grass! And if they mow the grass, they can't wear a hijab!" This obviously was a conflict she just couldn't tolerate. It's black and white, no grey. You're either all Muslim or no Muslim—at least for the hijab thing.

Appendix 4 Christians in Afghanistan

Almost all Afghan Christians are converts from Islam. The Pew Research Center estimates that 40,000 Afghan Christians were living in Afghanistan in 2010, or less than 0.1 percent of the population.[69] The VOA News estimates that Christians of Muslim background living in Afghanistan were between 500 and 8,000 in 2010.[70] And the International Religious Freedom Report estimates between 10,000 to 12,000.[71]

The latter two population estimates are also less than 0.1 percent of the population.

Reports indicate that the Taliban continues to persecute religious minorities and punish residents in areas under their control in accordance with their extreme interpretation of Islamic law," USCIRF said in a report. International Christian Concern (ICC), a U.S.-based non-government organization, says Afghan Christians are particularly under threat. "ICC is in direct communication with a number of families currently hiding from the Taliban. Some are in quite a serious situation, with the Taliban conducting sweeps of entire neighborhoods or districts," Claire Evans, ICC's Middle East program manager, told VOA. "They are deeply afraid and heavily targeted by the Taliban. If they are caught, their lives and that of their loved ones are at immediate risk," Evans said about Christians in Afghanistan.[72]

Even raising the topic of evacuation of Afghan Christians with Taliban officials will be problematic and potentially risky. "There are no Christians in Afghanistan. Christian minority has never been known or registered here," Inamullah Samangani, a Taliban spokesman, told VOA. "There are only

Sikh and Hindu religious minorities in Afghanistan that are completely free and safe to practice their religion," he added. Samangani did not specify what the Taliban would do if they find Afghans who have converted to Christianity, but quitting Islam has always been considered apostasy and punishable by law in Afghanistan. In 2006, an Afghan man, Abdul Rahman, who had converted to Christianity, was sentenced to death by a court in Kabul but flown to Italy after intense diplomatic pressure from the U.S. government.[73]

Figure 6. An imam speaks next to an armed Taliban fighter during Friday prayers at the Abdul Rahman Mosque in Kabul, following the Taliban's takeover of Afghanistan.[74]

Appendix 5 Geography

The only city in Afghanistan with over 1 million people is its capital, Kabul. The rest are smaller cities and towns. An estimated total number of people living inside Afghanistan was 32.2 million in 2020. Of this, around 7.8 million were reported to be living in urban areas and the rest in rural or countryside.[75] However, another source shows the population of Afghanistan at 39 million in 2023.[76] This difference is probably attributable to the difficulty of taking a census in Afghanistan.

Table 3. 18 cities of Afghanistan with a population over 100,000, by order of population.[77]

Name	Province	Population Estimates December 2022
Kabul	Kabul	3,500,000
Kandahar	Kandahar	651,484
Herat	Herat	592,902
Kunduz-i-Sharif	Balkh	500,207
Kunduz	Kunduz	268,893
Jalalabad	Nangarhar	280,685
Taloqan	Takhar	196,400

Name	Province	Population Estimates December 2022
Puli Khumri	Baghlan	221,274
Lashkargah	Helmand	276,831
Sheberghan	Jowzjan	175,599
Ghazni	Ghazni	190,424
Khost	Khost	160,214
Chaghcharan	Ghor	150,892
Mihtarlam	Laghman	144,162
Farah	Farah	590,000

Figure 7. Asadabad, capital of Kunar Province in the east.[78]

Figure 8. Kabul.[79]

Figure 9. Kandahar.[80]

Note the six countries adjacent to Afghanistan illustrated in Figure 12, making it land-locked, meaning it does not border a major water body. Afghanistan borders China in the northeast for less than 50 miles in an area known as the Wakhan Peninsula which is the highest mountains on earth and very sparse population.

National Highway 01 or National Highway 01, or NH01, formally called the Ring Road, is a 2,200 kilometers (1,400 miles) is a two-lane road network circulating inside Afghanistan, connecting ten major cities show on Figure 12. Kunduz is a six-hour bumpy road trip to Kabul, which Maryam travelled on in Chapter 1. It is the longest rote of the Asian Highway Network.[81]

Part of National Highway 01 has been refurbished since late 2003 particularly the Kabul-Kandahar Highway with funds provided by the United States, Saudi Arabia, and others. Most work on that stretch was done by Turkish, Indian, and local companies. Japanese companies were also involved near the southern Afghan province of Kandahar. In the west, Iran participated in the two land road construction between Islam

Qala and the western Afghan city of Herat. Pakistan rebuilt the
Jalalabad-Kabul Road.[82]

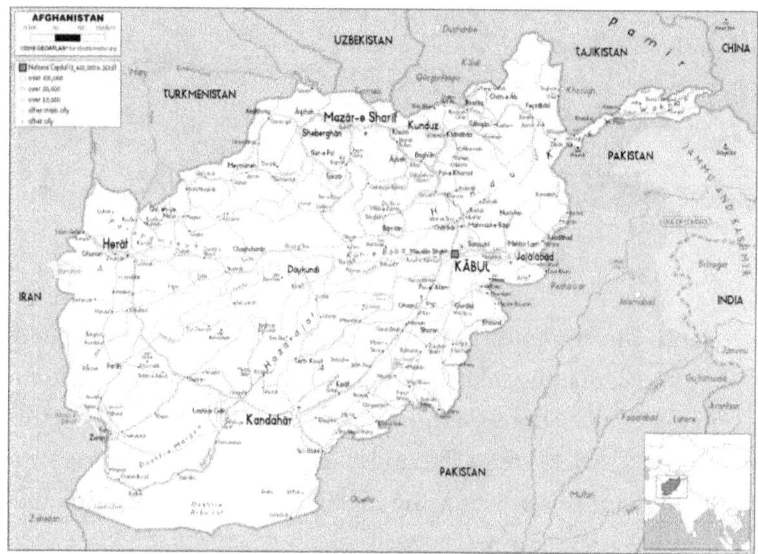

Figure 12. Afghanistan City and Road Map.[83]

Figure 11. Kabul–Jalalabad Road.[84]

Figure 12. Kabul–Kandahar Highway in Wardak Province, 2010.[85]

Kunduz is a city in northern Afghanistan, the capital of Kunduz Province. The city has an estimated population of about 269,000 as of 2015, making it the 7th-largest city of Afghanistan. As of 2015, the land use of the city is largely agricultural, nearly 66 percent of total area within the municipal boundary.[86] In the early 20th century, Kunduz became one of the wealthiest Afghan provinces. This was mainly due to the founding of the Spinzar Cotton Company, which continues to exist in post-war Afghanistan. At its peak, the Spinzar Cotton Company employed 5,000 people full time. Kunduz is the most important agricultural province, which produces wheat, rice, millet, and other products and obtained the nickname of "the hive of the country."[87] This city is famous in Afghanistan for its watermelon.

Kunduz is the site of the ancient city of Drapsaka. It was a great center of Buddhist learning and very prosperous during the 3rd century AD. It was ruled by various powers through the centuries, was captured by the Taliban in 1997, and was the last major city held by the Taliban before its fall to US-backed Afghan Northern Alliance forces in November 2001.[88]

Following that it endured fighting between the Taliban and U.S.-led forces until the Taliban takeover in August 2021.

Figure 13. Agricultural area of Kunduz.[89]

Figure 14. The Blue Mosque, Mazār-e Sharīf, Afghanistan.[90]

The Blue Mosque is one of the most important in Afghanistan and is known throughout the Muslim world. It is located in Kunduz-i-Sharif is a city in northern Afghanistan, 35 miles south of the border with Uzbekistan and a six hour drive south to Kabul. The city derives its name meaning "tomb of the saint" from the reputed tomb of the caliph ʿAlī, son-in-law of the Prophet Muhammad, over which a blue-tiled mosque and shrine were erected in the 15th century. Afghan tradition holds that the tomb was first discovered by revelation in the 12th century, and the original shrine was destroyed after the Mongol invasion in the 13th century.[91]

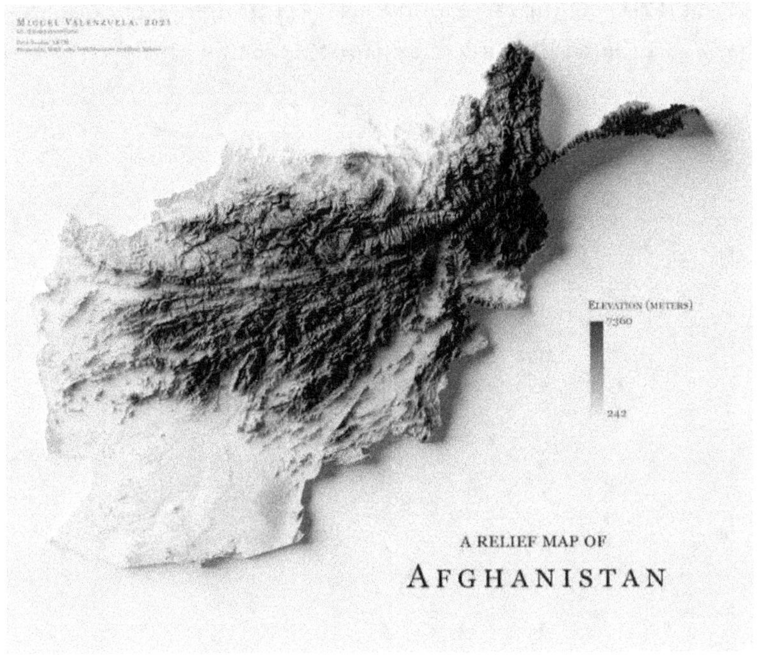

Figure 15. Afghanistan Relief Map.[92]

Over half of the land area of Afghanistan is mountainous, as illustrated in Figure 10. The mountains range from 3,300 feet to 23,000 feet (1,000 to 7,000 meters). The First Anglo-Afghan War was fought between the British Empire and the Emirate of Kabul from 1838 to 1842.[93] The Second Anglo-Afghan War was a military conflict fought between the British Raj and the Emirate of Afghanistan from 1878 to 1880.[94] The Soviets fought in the 1980's to overtake Afghanistan. The U.S. and allied forces from 2002 to 2021 tried to overcome the

Taliban. Each failed and left. A critical strategic advantage was their ability to hide in the mountains. External forces have ravaged Afghanistan going back to 1838. Also, Afghanistan suffered its own internal conflicts off and on throughout the 19th and 20th centuries. Continuous war through recent decades has exacerbated the violence against Afghan women.

End Notes

1 SafeHouse Center SPEAKS OUT,
https://www.safehousecenter.org/category/shc-speaks-out/,
accessed February 21, 2023.
21.40 births per woman (2020).
https://www.google.com/search?q=fertillity+rate+for+canada&rl
z=1C1JZAP_enUS1010US1010&oq=fertillity+rate+for+canada&
aqs=chrome..69i57j0i13i512j0i22i30l2j0i15i22i30j0i22i30l2j0i15i22i
30l3.7575j1j7&sourceid=chrome&ie=UTF-8. Accessed April 24,
2023
3 Afghanistan Fertility Rate 1950-2023.
https://www.macrotrends.net/countries/AFG/afghanistan/fertilit
yrate#:~:text=The%20fertility%20rate%20for%20Afghanistan,a%
203.41%25%20decline%20from%202021. Accessed April 24, 2023
4 V.R. Kutty, et al. Journal of Health Service. 1993;23(2):373-86.
13HM-CQVW. DOI: 10.2190/9N4P-F1L2-13HM-CQVW.
https://pubmed.ncbi.nlm.nih.gov/8500953/#:~:text=Socioecono
mic%20status%20was%20found%20to,population%2C%20religio
n%2C%20and%20region. Accessed April 24, 2023.
5 Bessel A. van der Kolk, MD, The Body Keeps Score. Penguin
Books. 2015. Page 159. Copyrighted material summarized.
6 Van der Kolk, op. cit., page 121. Copyrighted material
summarized.
7 van der Kolk, Bessel A., op. cit., p. 72. Copyrighted material
summarized.
8 van der Kolk, op. cit., p. 164. Copyrighted material summarized.
9 Van der Kolk, op. cit., page 86. Copyrighted material summarized
10 Amish School Shooting, LancasterPA.com.
https://lancasterpa.com/amish/amish-forgiveness, accessed March
26, 2023.
11 Human Rights, United Nations Assistance Mission in
Afghanistan (UNAMA), Kabul. Office of the United Nations High
Commissioner for Human Rights, Geneva. Silence is Violence:
End the Abuse of Women in Afghanistan. 8 July 2009.
https://unama.unmissions.org/sites/default/files/vaw-
english_1.pdf, 7accessed November 26, 2022

12 Afghanistan Independent Human Rights Commission (AIHRC),
Violence Against Women In Afghanistan, 6 January 2013,

(Biannual report 1391).
https://www.refworld.org/docid/529744454.html, accessed 27 November 2022. Page 1

[13] AIHRC Op. Cit., Page 22.

[14] TrustLaw Poll: Afghanistan is most dangerous country for women. Thomson Reuters Foundation. 15 June 2011. https://news.trust.org/item/20110615000000-na1y8/, accessed November 26, 2022.

[15] Human Rights, UNAMA. Op. Cit. Page 19.

[16] Human Rights, UNAMA. Op. Cit. Page 51.

[17] Human Rights, UNAMA. Op. Cit. Page 4.

[18] Human Rights, UNAMA. Op. Cit. Page 22.

[19] UNIFEM Afghanistan Fact Sheet 2008. [United Nations Development Fund for Women]. http://afghanistan.unifem.org/media/pubs/08/factsheet.html, accessed November 29, 2022

[20] Human Rights Watch, World Report 2013, Afghanistan, Events of 2012. Pages 1, 2. N.Y., N.Y. Copyright. https://www.hrw.org/world-report/2013/country-chapters/afghanistan, accessed December 1, 2022. Copyrighted material summarized.

[21] New York Times, In Afghanistan, Women Betrayed. By Heather Barr. December 10, 2013. https://www.nytimes.com/2013/12/11/opinion/in-afghanistan-women-betrayed.html, accessed February 22, 2024. Copyrighted, material summarized.

[22] Noorjahan Akbar, No Justice for Rape Victims in Afghanistan, UN Dispatch. July 26, 2013. https://www.undispatch.com/no-justice-for-rape-victims-in-afghanistan/, accessed December 24, 2022.

[23] Human Rights, UNAMA, op. cit., page 2.

[24] Human Rights, UNAMA, op. cit., page 22.

[25] Human Rights, UNAMA, op. cit., page 23.

[26] Rachel Reid; et al. (6 December 2009). "We Have the Promises of the World - Women's Rights in Afghanistan". Human Rights Watch. Georgetown Institute for Peace, Women, and Security, New York. Copyright. Retrieved 22 April 2018. As quoted in Wikipedia, https://en.wikipedia.org/wiki/Rape_in_Afghanistan, accessed September 22, 2022

[27] AIHRC, op. cit.

[28] AIHRC, op. cit.

[29] Global Rights: Partners for Justice. Living with Violence: A National Report on Domestic Abuse in Afghanistan. Washington, DC. March 2008. https://www.humanitarianresponse.info/sites/www.humanitarianresponse.info/files/documents/files/Living. accessed December 1, 2022. Page 1.

[30] Reuters, Violence against Afghan women more frequent, brutal in 2013: official. By Jessica Donati. January 4, 2014. Copyright permission granted. https://www.reuters.com/article/us-afghanistan-women/violence-against-afghan-women-more-frequent-brutal-in-2013-official-idusbrea030a620140104, accessed April 1, 2024. Copyright permission granted.

[31] U.S. State Department. Bureau of democracy, human rights, and labor. 2021 country reports on human rights practices: Afghanistan. Executive summary. https://www.state.gov/reports/2021-country-reports-on-human-rights-practices/afghanistan/, 6th paragraph. Accessed November 26, 2022.

[32] Women for Afghan Women, email from Women for Afghan Women, November 23, 2022.

[33] United Nations Human Rights, Office of the High Commissioner, "We are Erased", October 12, 2022. https://www.ohchr.org/en/stories/2022/10/we-are-erased, accessed December 1, 2022. [no copyright noted]

[34] Global Rights: Partners for Justice. Op. cit., pages 11-16, 24.

[35] UNIFEM Afghanistan Fact Sheet. Op. cit.

[36] Footnote withheld.

[37] Human Rights, UNAMA, op. cit., pp. 1, 2, 6, 9, 18, 19, and 22.

[38] TrustLaw Poll: Afghanistan is most dangerous country for women. Thomson Reuters Foundation. 15 June 2011. https://news.trust.org/item/20110615000000 na1y8, accessed November 26, 2022

[39] Noorjahan Akbar, op. cit.40 Rachel Reid; et al., op. cit.

[40] Rachel Reid; et al., op. cit.

[41] Amnesty International, Urgent Action: 10-year-old Rape Survivor Faces "honor" killing. UA: 253/14 Index: ASA 11/013/2014 Afghanistan, 9 October 2014. https://www.amnesty.org/en/wpcontent/uploads/2021/07/asa110132014en.pdf, accessed December 1, 2022

[42] Human Rights Watch, We Have the Promises of the World: Women's rights in Afghanistan, N.Y., N.Y. 2009. https://www.hrw.org/sites/default/files/reports/afghanistan1209 web_0.pdf, accessed November 29, 2022. Pp. 6, 7, 12, 32, 49, and 56.

[43] Human Rights Watch, "I Had to Run Away: The Imprisonment of Women and Girls for 'Moral Crimes' in Afghanistan." 2012. https://www.hrw.org/report/2012.03/28/i had run away/imprisonment women and girls moral crimes Afghanistan, accessed February 22, 2024. Pp. 29-31, 34, 37, 58, 65, 66, and 94. Copyrighted material summarized.

[44] Human Rights Watch, World Report 2013, Op. cit.

[45] New York Times. In Afghanistan, Women Betrayed. Heather Barr. December 10, 2013. https://www.nyTimes.com/2013/12/11/opinion/in afghanistan women betrayed.html, accessed December 1, 2022. Copyrighted material summarized.

[46] AIHRC, op. cit., pp. 7, 14, 17, 19, and 23.

[47] U.S. State Department, Bureau of democracy, human rights and labor. Country Reports on human   rights practices for 2013: Afghanistan. Section 6. Discrimination, Societal Abuses, and Trafficking in Persons/Women. https://2009 2017.state.gov/j/drl/rls/hrrpt013humanrightsreprot/index.htm#section6women, accessed November 26, 2022

[48] Reuters 2013, op. cit.

[49] Amnesty International, "Afghanistan: Harrowing accounts emerge of the Taliban's reign of terror in Kunduz."   Amnesty International. 1 October 2015. https://www.amnesty.org/en/latest/press-release/2015/10/afghanistan-harrowing-accounts-emerge-of-the-talibans-reign-of-terror-in-kunduz/, accessed December 24, 2022

[50] U.S. State Department. Bureau of democracy, human rights, and labor. Op. cit.

[51] Women for Afghan Women. Op. cit.

[52] United Nations Human Rights, Office of the High Commissioner. Op. cit.

[53] United Nations Development Programme, Human Development Report 2020.

[54] UN Women, Global Database on Violence against Women: Afghanistan, 2020-2021. https://evaw-global-

database.unwomen.org/en/countries/asia/afghanistan, accessed December 26, 2022

55 Starnews, Associated Press, Ellen Knickmeyer. Taliban aid policy poses dilemma. Page 4A. January 16, 2023.

56 van der Kolk, op. cit., pp. 146-147. Copyrighted material summarized.

57 AP News, Rahim Faiez. March 8, 2023. Associated Press writer Edith M. Lederer at the United Nations   contributed to this report. https://apnews.com/article/taliban-afghanistan-women-rights-united-nations-591c39436d53f83e5a0c423c5e06891c, accessed June 16, 2023.

58 AP News, Rahim Faiez. Associated Press. Wilmington North Carolina Star News. And Summary report of country-wide women's consultations [in Afghanistan], UN Women, UN Migration. September 21, 2023. https://asiapacific.unwomen.org/sites/default/files/2023-09/summary-report_september-2023-women-consultations.pdf, accessed September 29, 2023.

59 World Bank, https://www.google.com/search?q=afghanistan+population&rlz=1C1JZAP_enUS1010US1010&oq=afghanistan+population&aqs=chrome..69i57j0i512l9.4834j0j15&sourceid=chrome&ie=UTF-8, accessed March 2, 2023

60 CEO Magazine, https://ceoworld.biz/2019/09/18/countries-with-the-largest-diaspora-population-in-the-world-2019/, accessed March 3, 2023

61 CEO Magazine, Op. cit.

62 Worldometer, https://www.worldometers.info/world-population/population-by-country/, accessed March 3, 2023.

63 Afghan diaspora, https://en.wikipedia.org/wiki/Afghan_diaspora, accessed February 23, 2023.

64 Photo: https://www.middleeasteye.net/news/norway-seeks-ban-burqas-classrooms, accessed April 16, 2024.

65 Kate Clark and Sayeda Rahimi, We need to breathe too: Women across Afghanistan Navigate the Taleban's Hijab Ruling. Afghanistan Analysts Network. 1 Jun 2022. https://www.afghanistan-analysts.org/en/reports/rights-freedom/we-need-to-breathe-too-women-across-afghanistan-navigate-the-talebans-hijab-

ruling%EF%BF%BC/#:~:text=%E2%86%912-
Whereas%20in%20much%20of%20the%20Arab%20and%20wider
%20Muslim%20world,head%20and%20body%20more%20fully,
accessed March 13, 2023.
[66] Photo: Female art students in Afghanistan,
https://en.wikipedia.org/wiki/Islamic_veiling_practices_by_count
ry#:~:text=In%20Afghanistan%2C%20the%20hijab%20is,and%2
0everywhere%2C%20including%20in%20schools, accessed April
16, 2024
[67] Photo: Burqas in Afghanistan,
2022.https://www.google.com/search?q=burqa+in+afghanistan&
rlz=1C1JZAP_enUS1010US1010&oq=burqa+in+afghanistan&aqs
=chrome..69i57j0i22i30l6j69i60.10328j0j7&sourceid=chrome&ie=
UTF-8#imgrc=Kx_7SA_LeyaluM&imgdii=R_YGieUnuEgdEM,
accessed March 13, 2023.
[68] Photo: Street market, 2022
https://www.google.com/search?q=street+market+in+afghanista
n&rlz=1C1JZAP_enUS1010US1010&oq=street+market+in+afgh
anistan&aqs=chrome..69i57j0i546l2j0i546i64912.12072j1j7&sourcei
d=chrome&ie=UTF-8#imgrc=2r34Eq11OsS0HM, accessed
March 28, 2023. Copyright 2022. Reprinted with permission.
[69] Global Christianity – A Report on the Size and Distribution of
the World's Christian Population, (PDF), accessed March 28, 2023.
Pew Research Center.
[70] The 2011 International Religious Freedom Report. Hearing
Before the Subcommittee on Africa, Global Health, and Human
Rights of the Committee on Foreign Affairs, House of
Representatives, One Hundred Twelfth Congress, First Session,
November 17, 2011. Original from University of California Press.
2018. p. 86. ISBN 9780160905346
[71] VOA News. Taliban Says No Christians Live in Afghanistan; US
Groups Concerned. 16 May 2022.
[72] VOA News. Op. cit. Copyrighted 2022. Reprinted with
permission.
[73] VOA News. Op. Cit. Copyrighted 2022. Reprinted with
permission.
[74] VOA News. Op. cit. Copyrighted 2022. Reprinted with
permission.
[75] "NSIA Population Estimates 2019-20" (PDF) Archived from the
original (PDF) on 2020-06-09 as quoted in

https://en.wikipedia.org/wiki/List_of_cities_in_Afghanistan, accessed March 12, 2023.

76 Worldometer, Op. cit.

77 "NSIA Population Estimates 2019-20", Op. cit.

78 Photo: Asadabad. List of Cities in Afghanistan, https://en.wikipedia.org/wiki/List_of_cities_in_Afghanistan, accessed March 13, 2023.

79 Photo: Kabul. List of Cities in Afghanistan, https://en.wikipedia.org/wiki/List_of_cities_in_Afghanistan, accessed March 13, 2023..

80 Photo: Kandahar. List of Cities in Afghanistan, op. cit.

81 "Application of Road Numbering System National Highway", Archived 2017-05-07 at Wayback Machine The Ministry of Public Works. October 16, 2015.

82 Afghanistan Ring Road, https://en.wikipedia.org/wiki/Afghanistan_Ring_Road, accessed March 12, 2023

83 Afghanistan City and Road Map, https://www.google.com/search?q=Afghanistan+City+and+Road+Map&rlz=1C1JZAP_enUS1010US1010&oq=Afghanistan+City+and+Road+Map&aqs=chrome..69i57j69i64.1460j0j7&sourceid=chrome&ie=UTF-8#vhid=LabJA1jTKl2XKM&vssid=l, accessed August 3, 2023.

84 Photo: Kabul-Jalalabad Rd. List of Cities in Afghanistan. Op. cit.

85 Photo: Kabul-Khandahar Highway. List of Cities in Afghanistan. Op. cit.

86 Kunduz, https://en.wikipedia.org/wiki/Kunduz, accessed March 13, 2023.

87 Afghanistan's Misguided Economy | Boston Review. Web.archive.org. 8 February 2014. Accessed 9 January 2023.As quoted in Wikipedia, https://en.wikipedia.org/wiki/Kunduz, accessed March 13, 2023.

88 Footnote withheld.

89 Photo: Agricultural Area of Kunduz. Phot of Dirk Haas of Germany. https://en.wikipedia.org/wiki/Kunduz#/media/File:Kunduz_River_valley.jpg, accessed March 13, 2023

90 Photo: The Blue Mosque. Mazār-e Sharīf, Afghanistan, https://www.britannica.com/place/Mazar-e-Sharif, accessed April 16, 2024.

[91] The Blue Mosque, Mazār-e Sharīf, Afghanistan, op. cit.
[92] Afghanistan Relief Map.
https://www.reddit.com/r/MapPorn/comments/p63axd/a relief
map showing the topography of Afghanistan/#lightbox, accessed
April 9, 2024
[93] First Anglo-Afghan War,
https://en.wikipedia.org/wiki/First_Anglo-Afghan_War, accessed
March 13, 2023.
[94] Second Anglo-Afghan War,
https://en.wikipedia.org/wiki/1Second_Anglo-Afghan_War,
accessed March 13, 2023.

www.ingramcontent.com/pod-product-compliance
Lightning Source LLC
Chambersburg PA
CBHW071559150726
48000CB00004B/1521